Praise for .

"Rachel's story reminds me that ... er overlooked, unseen or abandoned. As you read these poetic, authentic lines, they will flow off the page and into your heart, touching you with the love of Jesus.

I challenge you to read this and not be impacted by the realization that God is at work in your life and is writing a beautiful, unique story through you too."

Anne Calver, Unleashed

"*Friend of God* invites the reader to see God work in the ordinary and mundane. Rachel's story demonstrates a naturally supernatural God, who is looking for friends that will partner with him.

I am convinced that this hope-giving, gritty and engaging story will encourage the reader to see God at work in places they had not previously."

Steve Uppal, All Nations

FRIEND *of*
GOD

The miraculous life
of an ordinary person

RACHEL YARWORTH

Dedicated to God,
my friend –
You know I did this for You.

And to my Mum and Dad,
who always loved me
and believed in me as a writer.
I love you both so very much.

Contents

ACKNOWLEDGEMENTS

With thanks to Mike, Josh, Ben and Daniel - for being such an awesome family, for bearing with me through all my writerly challenges, and for trying not to distract me when hearing the words "Mum's trying to write!" You are my greatest blessings and I love you all with all my heart.

Thanks also to Liz Carter, Andrew Chamberlain and Charlotte Milburn for catching and supporting my vision and sharing your skills to make this book so much better than it was. You are all amazing! And to Ruth Leigh, Brendan Conboy and Rowena Cross for your continuing encouragement and answering my MANY practical questions, making the writing/publishing process so much less daunting. Without you all I'm sure I would not have made it this far.

Thanks to all my beta readers who generously gave their time and feedback to help me hone the focus of what I was trying to achieve: Rhonda Spero, Alex Banwell, Joy Vee, Joy

Margetts, Amy Fischer, Jo Regan – you are all godly and gifted people in your own right, and your willingness to contribute was both humbling and extremely helpful!

And thanks to all my other cheerleaders, every one of whom prayed for me and kept me going when I was tempted to quit: my Home Group family, the Company of Prophets and the Warrior Mums – and everyone who has given me a vote of confidence by following or commenting on my writer pages/website. You guys are the best!

Finally, thank you to everyone who appears in this book: for graciously letting me write about you, and for your part in my life story, I thank you from the bottom of my heart. And to those who know me in real life who don't appear in these pages: I simply couldn't fit all of my life into one book – and that wasn't the point of this project anyway – but I'm so glad you are part of my bigger story. Thank you for being in my life!

CHAPTER 1

My Beginning

I was born in the early 1970s in Stroud, Gloucestershire, a town nestled at the centre of five valleys in the beautiful English Cotswolds. I was the middle one of three siblings, with an older brother and a younger sister. My dad was tall, bearded, and imposing, a lover of amateur dramatics, and able to create just about anything; whether candles, model aeroplanes, or endless practical storage solutions. While strict in his expectations of our behaviour, he was often spontaneously generous and always ready to boast to others about every tiny achievement. My mum was quieter by nature, but the centre of our world; a beautiful redhead who Dad used to claim wore the first mini skirt in Stroud and who quite simply put her family first in all she did. Provider of cuddles, unfailingly fair, and always ready to laugh with us, she was our steady, guiding light.

My parents used to take us to a small, traditional church on Sunday mornings. This church was unusual in that it had its own stage and amateur dramatics group, which attracted my father. We joined the congregation when I was a toddler, and thus began the Sunday morning ritual of church attendance that was dwindling but still familiar to many in the seventies.

We would sit in the same pew most weeks, the three of us under strict instruction to be quiet and still – heaven forbid we should swing our legs! The minister was a kind and friendly man, but the service followed a not-very-inspiring-to-us pattern of hymns, notices, offering and sermon. We children were not expected to listen to the grown-ups' sermon but had our own age-appropriate Sunday School classes in adjoining rooms, to which we escaped with relief.

I'm sad to say I don't remember much about Sunday School except that it put me off orange squash and slightly stale biscuits for life. I did like the Bible stories that the teachers read to us, but even as a young child I somehow felt there was a gap between what they were teaching and how they were living. I don't mean to imply that they were hypocrites – I can only assume they were genuine in their faith, and I certainly have no reason to believe otherwise. But all I can remember is the vaguest of impressions that the Jesus they taught about did exciting miracles and changed the world with his bold message, whereas my teachers – to my childish and undiscerning mind – just seemed aged and boring. I wouldn't have been able to articulate it at the time, but I think I just didn't understand why we didn't see people radically healed and delivered in our church, like they were in Jesus' time (and, if I'm honest, that question still challenges me about Christian churches today).

I vividly remember one Sunday afternoon when I was seven years old. I was in the bedroom I shared with my little sister, but she wasn't there at the time, so I assume I had been sent upstairs on my own either because of some poor behaviour or to tidy it up. It was a spacious second-floor attic room with a window that overlooked the main road, our neighbours opposite, and the hills beyond. It had a cheerful yellow paint scheme, two beds with brightly flowered duvets, a whole wall of built-in toy cupboards, and a floor regularly strewn with multiple books, dolls and toys that should have been in the cupboards.

As I sat on my bed, reading one of my cherished books instead of tidying up, I started to experience a strange but overwhelming feeling that the God of the Sunday School Bible stories was not only real, but somehow present with me. Impulsively, I hid under my duvet. I wasn't trying to hide *from* God, it was more like hiding *with* him: this was a beautiful experience that made me instinctively want to shut everything else out, to treasure it and immerse myself in it. There, in my first ever 'secret place', experiencing that awareness of his very real presence, I whispered to God, "I believe in you. I want to live my life your way."

I stayed for a while – not hearing anything and not saying anything else – just enjoying the sense of my new friend's presence surrounding me. Eventually that awareness slowly faded, and I went back to my book. On the outside I was just the same as before, but on the inside, I felt changed. I belonged to God. I didn't tell my family because I was worried that they might tell me I was too naughty for this to be true, but he was my secret friend, and I kept that secret for almost a decade.

Not long after that encounter something happened which confirmed to me that my new friend was looking after me. I was in my bedroom again, trying to reach something from the back of my wardrobe. It was an old, slightly battered wardrobe, but in my eyes still beautiful: made of mahogany with carved decorations, a deep drawer at the base with metal rings for handles, a large oval mirror in the front door, with two hanging rails inside on either side of the door and several coat hooks around the top, too high for me to reach. My dad had repeatedly told us children NOT to climb inside the wardrobe. As a lover of C.S. Lewis' *Chronicles of Narnia*, I was frequently tempted to do so, to try to find a magical world beyond. But Dad had warned us with dark imaginings of the tragedy that would inevitably follow if we disobeyed. So, with my siblings and I having received dire warnings of being crushed or suffocated if we caused the wardrobe to fall on us, we mostly obeyed and stayed out. However, on this day there was something I particularly wanted, so I climbed in, reached up on my toes – and promptly felt my world lose all sense and stability as the wardrobe tipped over and came crashing to the ground. Stunned and disoriented, it took me a while to register what had happened – and then I was relieved to discover that although the wardrobe had indeed fallen and I was stuck inside it, I was in fact not dead. I gingerly felt my limbs, head and torso, but could not find any injury at all.

As my eyes slowly adjusted to the darkness around me, I spotted a sliver of faint light to one side. It seemed a good idea to head for that, so I wriggled and twisted and awkwardly inched towards it, until I finally found myself crawling out – from underneath my bed. There I found my whole white-faced family trying to comprehend the scene: my sister crying and clinging to my mum who was doing her best to reassure her, and my brother frozen in fear, anxiously watching my dad who was carefully trying to manoeuvre the wardrobe back to its feet. As waves of confusion and relief crossed their faces, I edged round the bed to their thankful embrace – and there I saw what had saved me: an old metal trunk that had originally belonged to my grandfather during his war-service, but which now contained our dressing-up clothes. It was usually kept well under my bed – the corners were quite sharp and painful if you accidentally walked into it – but for some reason today it was sticking out. It wasn't so far out as to barricade the fallen wardrobe's door shut with me inside, but just far enough that when the wardrobe fell adjacent to my bed, it landed with one edge on the metal trunk, allowing the door to open just enough for a child to squeeze through.

I didn't say anything to my family, but inside I had no doubt that God, my secret friend, had made sure the trunk was perfectly placed to save me that day. It wouldn't be the last time he saved me, either.

> *I was just a child – nobody important…*
> *BUT GOD (I love those two words: whenever they crop up in the story of my life, they invariably signify Him stepping in to rewrite the story in a beautiful way).*
> *… BUT GOD chose to be my friend.*

CHAPTER 2

Troubled Teen

Time went on, we children grew, and when I was 13 we moved house – not far away, but our involvement with the church fizzled out around that time. This was not due to any decision that I was aware of – I just noticed one day that we didn't really go anymore, and nobody seemed to miss it.

My teenage years were not very happy ones. I was highly sensitive and socially awkward – a gawky, painfully self-conscious teen who struggled to make friends, largely because of my insecurity and severe lack of confidence. I was at a grammar school for bright girls, but my classmates were just as capable of self-centeredness and unkindness as any other children. My entire class stopped speaking to me and ignored me for two whole years. I had no idea what I had done to cause it, but I was desperately unhappy. And, harder still for me, my dad – who held his opinions every bit as strongly as I did mine – found me difficult to deal with too. Despite being sensitive I had a deeply ingrained sense of right and wrong, just like him, and I was not the sort to keep quiet – whatever the cost – when I felt injustice was being done. We argued often, with periods of time when he did not know how to talk to me at all. My mum was still loving, only reprimanding me when I deserved it (not that I would have said so at the time), but I was painfully aware of their arguments about me; Dad frustrated and angry, Mum trying her best to plead my case. I felt responsible and withdrew, trying to protect them from the fall-out of my own struggles.

So, through a combination of my classmates' rejection, the conflict with my dad, and my own chaotic emotions, I came to believe I must be wrong in myself: too emotional, too difficult, and simply not good enough or nice enough as a person. I was convinced I did not belong and simply felt in the way. It was an intensely painful, lonely time.

One day at school, I started feeling hot and nauseous, so I laid my head down on my desk. A classmate came up to me and asked if I was okay. I jumped, startled. "I… I don't feel too good," I said, stumbling over my words, and she took my arm and led me to the school office where the receptionist took one look at me and promptly sent me home.

I had to take a previously longed-for day or two off to recover, but for the first time I looked forward to going back to school. Somebody had cared about me! I was so pathetically grateful to my classmate for simply noticing me that I started to do everything I could to please her.

She, like many of the girls in my class, used to catch the bus home from school. There were quite a few others who didn't need the bus but who would still walk into town together to hang out at the bus station, as a way of prolonging their enviable socialising. When my new friend invited me to join them, I couldn't believe it. I was wanted!

So, even though it was completely out of my way, I went. Initially we would just wait at the bus stop together. Many of them would smoke, but it never appealed to me – I just contented myself with occasionally holding their lit fags for them, thinking I looked 'cool'. Eventually, though, somebody would get bored. My friend liked wandering round the shops and I wondered if she was putting off going back to her foster family, but I gladly went with her even though I had no money to spend. Lack of funds didn't stop her, though; she decided to take me under her wing, giving me tips on how to stealthily slip things into a bag or pocket and then leave the shop without paying. At first I was horrified, but could not see past how 'kind' she was being to me, and before long I was joining her and sometimes her other friends on regular shoplifting sprees.

I knew it was wrong, but suppressed my conscience, burying it under the months and months of accumulated rejection and hurt. I had learned to switch off my emotions to survive, and denying my guilty feelings was a natural extension of denying my pain. I tried to convince myself I didn't care and did all I could to protect my desperately unhappy heart with a hard shell.

God, the secret friend of my childhood, seemed a distant memory – too far away to help me with all my feelings of confusion and rejection. And, as I had never told anyone of my faith, I had no spiritual friends or guides to take me under their wing and help me find my way. I was no longer conscious of God's loving presence and felt utterly lost.

At the height of my problems, age 15, I went abroad for two weeks as part of a school exchange programme with a German school. Removed from my everyday life, and far from my family (and my shoplifting cronies), my sense of lostness was unavoidable, and my deepest feelings of vulnerability intensified. The family I was staying with had an immaculate house. The stark white walls and perfectly polished surfaces reflected the inhabitants: impeccably polite and attractive, but to me at least, lacking the warmth and comfort of my own family. How I needed just a little mess, a minor flaw to reassure me that the chaos of my internal self wasn't wholly out of place. Only one of the family spoke English but he was rarely there, and I was far too self-conscious to try to communicate in their native language (even though that was the very reason I was there). Cut off from anyone to talk to, and in surroundings that made me feel even more out of place, I was very homesick. Without healthy coping mechanisms, my default was to try to suppress my feelings and try my hardest to 'not care'. But once alone, I couldn't pretend. There was something about those spotless surroundings, combined with the intense longing for those at home, that opened my heart to the realisation of how disappointed my parents would be if they knew about the shoplifting.

Then one night, as I struggled to sleep in the immaculate guest room, feeling utterly alone and undeserving of love, the divine presence I had encountered eight years before came to me once again, surrounded me with love and gently 'told me' (i.e. convinced my heart as surely as if someone had spoken out loud) that what I was doing – stealing – was wrong and I needed to stop. It was one tiny moment in time; no angelic visitation or dramatic sign, just a simple, subtle awareness of his presence with me that drew me back to his love. Sometimes it's the small, invisible details that can change whole lives.

I made the decision there and then, and simply stopped. There was no sense of shame, chastisement, ridicule, or emotional manipulation from God. In that simple encounter, he reminded me that he loved me, helped me to acknowledge and turn my back on my mistakes, and drew me back to friendship with him. My heart felt clean again, and free.

I was loved.

On returning home, I did indeed stop shoplifting, but those I had been hanging around with did not. The police discovered them, and without hesitation my 'friend' blamed me. Of course, my parents then found out too, and one of the biggest regrets of my life is the pain I caused them at that time, especially for my mum, who had to seek help from her work colleagues (she was a legal secretary) – how humiliating that must have been.

But, although my relationship with my dad had been rocky, neither he nor my mum rejected me. After the initial police visit, I broke down in tears. "You won't love me anymore," I cried.

Mum sat down next to me, firmly grasped my hands, and emphatically declared, "Rachel, you are our daughter – we will NEVER stop loving you."

As I sobbed in her arms, her words – and actions – of unconditional love sank into me like a deeply healing balm, soothing my inner turmoil. And when the time came for me to go to receive my official caution, Dad came to the police station with me, keeping my hand in his as we walked in. I remember waiting for what seemed like ages in the little windowless room. A stern-looking officer came in and sat behind the huge desk, then looked straight at me as he emphasised the seriousness of my actions. "Are you truly sorry, Rachel?" he said, his grave eyes fixed on mine.

For a moment, I struggled to speak, but finally found my voice. "Yes," I said clearly, nodding firmly.

Through the whole experience – the wait and the lecture – I was a mess of emotions: embarrassment, humiliation, fear, and shame. But through it all I could feel my dad's solid and comforting presence by my side, and I knew that although we had our clashes and misunderstandings, beneath it all he loved me still. Regardless of our difficulties, when I was in my darkest place, I was thankful to realise I had the unconditional love of a good father.

It was not long afterwards that, aged 16, I decided it was time to stop hiding my secret. I revealed my beliefs by asking my dad to make me a wooden cross in his workshop so I could hang it above my bed. He gladly did so.

Soon after that we had another argument. I can't remember what it was about – despite our renewed connection I was still a hormonal teenager and both of us were still opinionated; we clashed regularly, especially if I felt he was being unfair or unjust. It may have been just my arguing back that he deemed to be naughty at that point, or he may have been referring to my previous shoplifting, or any number of other perceived misdemeanours. Whatever the reason, my fear from years ago of being labelled 'not good enough' for the God I loved was coming true: "You can't call yourself a Christian," I remember him declaring, "You do too many bad things."

If I'd heard those words as a seven-year-old from someone I loved, I would have been crushed and probably given up on my friendship with God. But now, as a strong-willed and opinionated teenager, I shrugged, brushing off my dad's comment. *What does he know? I'll prove him wrong*, I thought.

My motives were rubbish, but my friendship with God was established and no longer a secret.

I was lost in pain and wrongdoing...
BUT GOD found me and brought me back to Him.

CHAPTER 3

Clueless But Protected

My friendship with God was now rekindled, but I didn't go back to church. The religion of church services still seemed completely distinct from and unrelated to the friendship I had with God. I thought of myself as a Christian but didn't know any other Christians like me who simply loved God and felt loved by him.

I still felt like I didn't quite belong anywhere.

However, things were looking up at school. In sixth form, the classes were juggled around to allow for the many who had left at 16 and the few who had joined the rest of us for A levels. So now I was in a new class with lots of girls I had never met. Boosted by my renewed friendship with God, I vowed not to repeat the mistake of trying to please others to gain their friendship, and I seized the opportunity for a fresh start. I decided that I was going to try to just be me, and if nobody liked me, at least I would have some self-respect. I found the things that appealed to me: joining the school choir and drama clubs, and organising fundraising activities for charities that I cared about. Most importantly, rather than waiting for people to be friendly to me, I made the most of some new-found acting skills to assume a confidence that didn't come naturally, and went out of my way to be friendly to others, especially those who looked friendless – after all, I had first-hand experience of what a lonely place that could be.

And suddenly everyone wanted to be my friend. I was voted form captain and awarded lots of badges, given solos at concerts and leading roles in plays. I even met my first boyfriend, who didn't last long but was kind and respectful, and I remember him with real fondness. I was now popular – and it really messed with my head.

Of course, I enjoyed it – it was so much nicer to have people now praising or wanting to hang out with me – but I didn't understand it, and it all felt rather unstable. I was grateful, but also confused and sometimes angry, and I experienced a bout of depression that I couldn't explain at the time. The more people seemed to want to be my friend, the more it rubbed up against my subconscious belief that I was somehow wrong in myself, and I kept expecting them to find me out and reject me as had happened before.

God was firmly established in my mind as my friend, but I didn't know how to ask him for help, and I still didn't know anyone who could help me with that. Prayer was a mystery. And the real question that I wanted to ask him, but didn't have the confidence to express, was why he made me this way: highly sensitive, yet longing to speak out for justice and truth, the combination of which caused so much deeply painful conflict. It seemed to be more of a curse than a blessing.

But I didn't want to lose his friendship again, so I suppressed my deepest questions and muddled along for a couple more years, not exactly praying as most Christians would recognise it, but just talking to God from time to time, hoping he was listening. I may have had a Bible, but I don't remember reading it; I preferred a cartoon-style book of Bible stories called *The Real Jesus* bought with a book token won in Sunday School years before.

So, I knew God loved me, but I had no idea how to get to know him better. I resigned myself to a life of simply trusting in a loving but distant God. Despite my ignorance, though, he used an incident from those years to demonstrate again his desire to be 'hands-on', not distant...

When I was 16, I got a Saturday job stacking shelves in a local supermarket. Most of the Saturday staff were the same age as me, and we all got on well enough. I still felt self-conscious and socially awkward, but was learning how to act the part of an extrovert – plus they were an outgoing, friendly bunch, so although I didn't exactly fit in, we managed fine. After I had worked there for a while, we were joined by a new, older girl with a thin, sensitive face and a nervous smile. She was only a few years older – barely into her twenties – but she was married, which made her a bit of an alien to the rest of us. She seemed too young to hang out with the older women on staff, but being married endowed her with an aura of life experience that none of us teens could relate to. I recognised a fellow loner, though, someone else who didn't seem to fit in, so I tried to be kind to her.

One day, after a few weeks of persisting through excruciatingly polite conversations, she suddenly asked if I would like to go for a meal with her and her husband. As an awkward teenager this seemed in the realm of adulthood and not at all appealing to me, but I didn't feel able to refuse, especially as I had made the effort to befriend her. Above all, I didn't want her to feel rejected, and felt this would be a good opportunity to practise my new confident, outgoing persona. So I agreed and we set the date.

The day came and we finished work, changed out of our ugly nylon uniforms, and travelled back to her house where her husband joined us for a mediocre meal and a game of *Trivial Pursuit*. Even in her own home my new friend didn't seem to relax. She remained quiet and awkward, with only an occasional nervous smile. Her charming husband, a good bit older than her with greying temples and an easy smile, was more talkative and asked me lots of questions about myself – a very attentive host. Nonetheless, I was grateful for the board game, which almost distracted me from the strange, uncomfortable, niggling sensation I had tried to suppress all evening, telling myself I was being silly when these two were such a nice couple. But even with all my efforts to calm my irrational emotions I kept finding myself internally counting down the time until I could get away. I managed to win the game and the husband expressed his admiration of my intelligence. It was flattering but made me even more uneasy, especially as I wondered how my friend felt about his lack of compliments towards her.

Next, they asked me if I wanted a tour of the house, so I politely agreed; anything to fill the time until I could leave! I thought their circular bed with its red satin sheets seemed odd and impractical, but nothing else was notable, so I made politely appreciative noises until I felt it was an acceptable time to ask for a lift home.

At home, I sagged with relief, vowing never to do that again. Nothing bad had happened, but I just felt strange and on edge the whole time, even though I couldn't have said why. I put it down to my permanent internal awkwardness and forgot about it.

Months later, the extent of my naivety was revealed when my Mum read out an account in the town newspaper of a local couple who had been found guilty of seducing (nowadays we would call it grooming) underage girls into taking part in threesomes. Their method was to befriend these girls through the wife's succession of work contacts. Once home they would have a meal, play a game of *Trivial Pursuit* and all end up in the bedroom – on that awful, impractical circular bed!

To this day I have no idea why they let me go home without pursuing anything further, other than that God was protecting me. I was very naïve, and it didn't occur to me to pray about my uneasy feelings; I just assumed I was being silly. Nowadays I would recognise my unease as God clearly trying to warn me, but at the time I just wasn't experienced enough in hearing his voice to realise it.

I was utterly ignorant of the danger I had put myself in…
BUT GOD protected me.

CHAPTER 4

Finding My Tribe

Ever since my very first days at primary school, I had one ambition: to be a teacher. I loved children, and I relished the satisfaction of helping them to grow and learn new things. When I got to secondary school, I worked out what qualifications I needed to go to teacher training college, and despite the challenges of my social and emotional struggles, I managed to learn just enough to achieve the requisite grades. I didn't want to go far away as a student, just far away enough to be independent, but near enough to my family for it to be easy to get home when I wanted. There were three teacher training colleges that met those criteria, but I couldn't choose between them, even after I had visited them. In the end my decision was made based on the glossy prospectus that looked most appealing – an illogical instinct rather than considered reason. I don't think I prayed about it: I was now practised at praying for help if my loved ones or I were in trouble, but I wasn't used to asking God specific questions, and I certainly didn't expect to hear any answers. However, my application led to an interview which went well: they accepted me provisionally, I achieved the necessary grades, and off I went to college at Oxford.

I moved onto campus in a house of about ten girls, where just along the corridor from my room was the friendliest girl I had ever met. She was warm and vibrant and seemed genuinely pleased to meet me. It turned out she was on the Christian Union committee. I didn't have any plans to join the CU (I still thought of most Christians as people who I didn't really identify with), but this girl Alison seemed to glow with life, so I thought I might as well tag along just to see what it was like. Not only did she invite me to the CU freshers' event, but before we got there something happened to someone who she was planning to perform a short sketch with, and she was left looking for a new partner who could act. She discovered that I had been involved in drama while in sixth form, so asked if I would help her out. It seemed like a minor thing to me, and I gladly agreed. Thus I was effectively plunged right into the middle of CU life from the very start of my college years. I hadn't realised when I applied, but this college had a disproportionately large CU – the second largest society in the college – and was exactly what I needed for encouragement in my faith.

Everyone in the Christian Union saw me and seemed to accept me, and from that point on I was fully immersed. I made many new friends there, some of whom invited me to go with them to different church services, and through those visits I found two churches who spoke about Jesus like he was their friend, the same way I knew him! It was so exciting. I went regularly to both churches; one on Sunday mornings and the other in the evenings. Being in Oxford, both churches had thriving student communities that felt so much more relatable than the mostly elderly congregations of my childhood. Not only that, but the services were very different too: they prayed for the sick, prophesied[1], sang, danced, and had fun! In church! This was a far more appealing brand of Christianity. And it wasn't just the churches providing me with space to learn and grow in faith. The college CU had weekly meetings where many visiting speakers came to encourage us. I remember a few speakers who made a lasting impact...

There was one who spoke about the father heart of God. It was quite near the beginning of the year, and I was enjoying my new-found independence and success at projecting a confident persona to those around me. As usual we sang a couple of worship songs and then all sat down to listen to the speaker. He had kind eyes that twinkled above his bearded smile, and a warm tone of voice that was very easy to listen to. For some reason he singled me out just after he started, declaring I was good at maintaining eye-contact with him while he preached. He thanked me for encouraging him this way, and then it became a kind of running joke through the message as he would periodically check that I was still following, interrupting his talk to ask, "You still with me, Rachel?"

---

[1]*Prophesied* – gave a prophecy, which is speaking out God's divine insight about something that is going to happen or that He wants us to know

To begin with it was easy to laugh along with him, but as the message continued, I became more and more uncomfortable. His message was a positive one, about God being our loving father, but the more he spoke, the more I was being internally assaulted by long-suppressed emotions associated with my human dad, who I knew loved me but whom I also felt I had disappointed. So for me, to name God as a loving father brought me face to face with feelings of total inadequacy as a daughter. Those locked-away feelings of shame and rejection grew internally louder and louder until it was all I could do to stay in the room, let alone look at the speaker. The last time he asked if I was still with him, I think I managed a kind of strangled yelp of agreement, and then I just had to hold onto my seat to make it to the end. It didn't occur to me to quietly slip out of the room to avoid the subject, so I stayed and heard his whole message of the unconditional love and acceptance of our Heavenly Father.

And the wounds I had picked up from some of the misunderstandings with my earthly dad were exposed.

I wasn't yet able to process all my internal pain immediately – it would take a while to fully heal – but that day of acknowledging my pain and mess in front of God was the beginning of the path to internal healing that over the next few years came to result in a restored, healthy and strong relationship with my dad.

After that meeting, the CU hosted a couple who came and spoke about miracle healing – how Jesus is still alive today, and still as willing to heal as he was when he walked on earth. I had only had experience of asking God to heal loved ones on two occasions when I was younger: once was when my Gran had a bad back, and I hid under my duvet and secretly asked God to make her better. She got better, and my childish confidence was boosted. But the second time, when my Grampie was taken gravely ill with cancer, I prayed again, and the next day he seemed to get better, but the day after that he died. I lost my confidence and didn't pray for healing again... until that CU meeting.

At the time, my sister was quite unwell at home. I was becoming more familiar with visiting speakers, so after this particular meeting I approached one of them to ask if she would pray for my sister. As she prayed, she prophesied over me that I would be involved in a healing ministry myself. I turned hot then cold as my stomach started churning with a strange mixture of excitement and confusion. Although I was learning that there was more to Christianity than I had known before, I felt like those who seemed to have a deeper faith were on a different level, unattainable to me, and the thought of having any kind of ministry seemed far too grand for somebody like me. So, I asked God that if the prophecy was true, would he please confirm it when I got back to my room?

I intended to read the Bible that one of my new friends had given me but was distracted on the way back to my room and forgot all about it. Much later I picked up a Lewis Carroll anthology that I was studying, and it happened to fall open at a poem about Florence Nightingale. All the thoughts and distractions in my mind suddenly stopped as I remembered my request to God for confirmation. I haven't been able to find the poem since, but right then it jumped out at me that it was about a lady of healing. I felt a certainty that God was getting my attention, not only answering my prayer and letting me know that healing would be part of my future ministry, but also affirming that he does speak through prophecy!

Perhaps most important to my relationship with God was the person who came and spoke about the Holy Spirit[2], whom I had not really heard about before. Either I wasn't paying attention very well or they were deliberately vague about the subject of their talk, perhaps trying to respect all the different church backgrounds represented there, because I didn't fully grasp their message. All I understood was that they spoke about a power available to all Christians that would enable us to live the kind of powerful life that Jesus intended. And they invited all who were interested to come to the side of the room for them to pray with. So I did – it seemed like a no-brainer to me: who wouldn't want God's power in their lives, helping them to know him better? As they prayed for me and the others who responded, I felt a kind of inner warmth and felt a bit drunk – full of joy.

A few days later in a church service, the congregation were invited to speak in tongues[3] if they could. In the traditional church of my childhood, speaking in tongues had never been mentioned even as a possibility. It was only now as a student that I became aware of it, both in the CU and at the new churches I had joined – including the Church of England one. And because it was clearly written about in the Bible, I gladly told God that I would quite like that gift. I felt that same sense of warmth and joy wash over me, and decided it was worth a try. So I opened my mouth to speak, and asked God to fill my

[2] *Holy Spirit* – one third of the Trinity; God as He lives and moves among us on Earth
[3] *Speak in tongues* – to speak in an earthly or heavenly language unknown to the speaker, as empowered by the Holy Spirit

mouth with His heavenly language. And he did. It was a lovely experience, but there was just one thing that bothered me, and that was that it didn't seem like a huge powerful thing, just a kind of babbling. It reminded me of when my sister and I were children and we used to pretend we were speaking in a foreign language. I worried that maybe I wasn't really speaking in tongues but making it up, so I told God my worries and asked him for guidance.

Soon after that, I read in the Bible that the Holy Spirit intercedes for us through 'groanings that cannot be uttered'[4], and that God sees our hearts and receives the desires of the Spirit in accordance with his plan for us. I felt an instant peace and knew then that it didn't matter what words I used, as God hears the prayers of our hearts and the Spirit. I didn't need to hear an audible voice – in my heart I was completely reassured and confident that whether I spoke in English or tongues or even made-up babble, the Holy Spirit could and would take my heart's desire for God and communicate it straight to the Father. So, the pressure of 'getting it right' was lifted immediately.

Being filled with the Holy Spirit happened just as naturally and without ceremony – without me realising exactly what had happened – as when I became friends with God as a child. In fact, it took a campus mission for me to understand the significance of that childhood commitment. The CU committee had organised a campus mission with visiting ministers every evening over several days. There was a pair of musicians with guitars who led us in singing enthusiastic worship songs, and a gifted speaker who boldly preached the Good News about

[4] Romans 8:26

Jesus: that he is the Son of God, born on earth as a man to take the eternal death sentence due to us as sinners, and to make a way for us to live in eternal friendship with God. At the end of each evening, the speaker invited anyone who believed to be 'born again'. It was the first time I had heard the phrase, and I was troubled by it. If I hadn't had this experience, was I even a Christian?

By now I was confident in my friendship with Jesus and agreed with all that these people said about him, and I understood the concept of starting a new spiritual life, but I had never had the conversion experience they spoke of: confessing sin, repenting, and accepting Jesus as Lord[5] – so maybe I wasn't 'born again'? My friend noticed that I was bothered, and when I explained why, she wisely said, "Well, if you're worried about *not* being born again, why don't you do it now?" I dutifully prayed the prayer as advised, but I didn't notice any real difference afterwards, and wondered why not. After all, the visiting ministers had spoken about how becoming Christians made a dramatic difference to their lives. Why wasn't I experiencing that?

Eventually I asked God about it. At this point, prayer for me was still mostly a one-way conversation of requests and general questions, for which I hoped he might be able to get the answers to me somehow. On occasion I had felt an undefinable but certain assurance that can only have come from him, but overall, I still had very little experience of recognising when he was talking to me.

---

[5] Being 'born again' to new spiritual life takes a process of a) *Confessing sin*, or acknowledging the wrong in our lives, b) *Repenting*, which is simply choosing to turn away from our wrongdoings or sin – and c) *Accepting Jesus as Lord* – expressing the belief that Jesus paid the penalty for our sin, and committing our lives to following him

However, this time, for the first time I saw a clear picture – a kind of mental image – in response to my question. And the picture that clearly and suddenly came to mind was of me as a seven-year-old, hiding under my duvet and whispering my childish prayer of commitment to him. As soon as I saw that image, I knew he was talking to me, showing me the moment I became his own, and that even though I didn't know the term 'born again' when I was seven, and didn't have full theological understanding of what I had done, he knew my heart. He reassured me that I really was his friend forever.

So now, after the long childhood years of isolated Christianity with no-one around me to share my friendship with God with, I was surrounded by abundant blessings provided during my time among new friends at Oxford. But there was one more blessing to come that I hadn't known I needed. While I was at college there were changes happening back at home, too. My sister had been impacted by the faith I was now freely enjoying, and she had made her own decision to follow Jesus. A friend of hers from school had invited her to a service at her church in our hometown, Stroud, and my sister had enjoyed it so much she kept going. My parents, however, were concerned. Their only experience of church was of a traditional one with pews, hymns, and an organist. The one my sister was getting involved in was something altogether different, with guitars, dancing, and open-air preaching – they didn't even have their own steepled building, but rented a room at the town hall! My parents called me to express their concerns that it might be a cult and asked me if I would go along when I was next home. I gladly agreed – I always had been very protective of my little sister – and so next time I went home I visited her new church with her. There I was delighted to meet a new group of people who were friends with God, just like me, but in our hometown!

They were, of course, not a cult, but a lively, healthy church – and not only that, but they were part of the group of churches that one of my Oxford churches belonged to!

I had been friends with God on my own for over ten years and made some foolish mistakes along the way, but he had never let me go. And now, aged eighteen, encouraged by the churches, the preaching, and my experiences with God at college, I finally found a church family where I belonged. I had found my tribe.

I never realised how much I needed other Christians around me...
BUT GOD did, and he knew exactly how to get me to them!

CHAPTER 5

The Man of my Dreams

I was still away at college for most of the time, but when I was home for the holidays, I was excited to have a place that accepted and encouraged me in my friendship with God. I felt I belonged at last! And it was during my first summer holiday at home that I met a man who would become very important to me.

We met at a friend's 'Hat and Boot' themed 18th birthday party. I was very happy to wear a hat, but while I had a selection of hats to choose from, I had no boots at all – in those days I walked barefoot nearly everywhere I went, in a small attempt to assert my individuality (also I hated shoe-shopping). So I only managed half of the theme, but, having grown in confidence by being away at college and the acceptance from my new church family, I went anyway. People appreciated my hat and generously smiled with me about my lack of boots, and all was well.

The party was underway, and we had spilled out into the garden when I heard the hostess scream. We all turned, and I saw a young man wearing boots on his feet and carrying a strategically placed hat in front of him, which was important because apart from those two items he appeared to be stark naked (I later discovered he did actually have a pair of swim-trunks on to protect his modesty, but initially those weren't obvious behind the hat). My first thought was "What a poser!" and I turned my back to continue chatting with my friends.

At some point, I was introduced to the poser and learned his name was Mike. He says of that first meeting that he thought I was interesting, and that was about it for both of us. Imagine my surprise when I went to church that Sunday and found the poser there – thankfully with all his clothes on!

Over the summer we got to know each other better, which was helped in part by our church leader putting out an appeal for some men to help on the PA desk, with training given if needed. I was still an opinionated individual and was irritated by the perceived inference that only men could do it. I wasn't badly offended, but I did want to make my point, so I volunteered. They gladly accepted (not actually being as sexist as the announcement sounded), and I received training to operate the desk from the head of the PA team... Poser Mike!

So inside church as well as outside with a group of mutual friends, Mike and I saw quite a lot of each other. I learned he was a lot of fun, smart, and caring, and by the time I went back to college we were firm friends. Over the following year we stayed in touch and reconnected easily whenever I came home.

In my first year at college, I had had a relationship with a fellow student that didn't end well and left me hurt, so I was not in the mood for romance. However, it had motivated me to draw up a list of the things I would want in a future boyfriend/ possible husband. I didn't see the point in putting myself through the heartbreak of dating someone who I wasn't potentially going to marry, so I drew up my list of things to pray for once I was ready. I don't remember much of what was on the list, but I do know that top of the list was that he had to be friends with Jesus too. Then it was the usual shallower stuff of tall, dark, handsomeness – preferably with meltingly brown eyes – and a few more ideals besides.

One day during the second summer I was home from college, Mike and I were chatting in my parents' kitchen about our lists (all the young Christian singles had similar lists in those days), and as we chatted, I started to feel a bit freaked out that Mike's list and mine were so well-matched. As I still wasn't looking for a relationship, I thought to myself, "I know what will put him off," and I pulled out my trump card. For some reason I had decided that I wanted a large family – six children, to be precise. So, I asked him if having children was on his list, and he promptly replied, "Yes – I want six!"

I tried to keep a neutral face but inside I was shocked. I felt that God was showing me the man who I would one day marry, even though I wasn't ready at that point.

That summer we saw a lot of each other. We worked together in a coffee bar for teens, I helped Mike set up his first flat, and we spent lots of our spare time together. By the end of the holiday we were very close, and people were talking. It was friendly talk from our church family who all loved us both and wished us to be happy together, but it was bothering Mike. Just before I went back to college, we went for a late evening walk on the common near my house and talked.

"I really like you, Rachel," he said, "but I don't want to be in an official relationship right now, just because everyone around us seems to expect it…" He paused. "Could we just stay friends?"

I swallowed, because deep down my heart was breaking. I knew in that moment that despite not wanting a relationship I had still fallen in love with him. But I could see he was upset, so I tried to comfort him. "Don't worry, I understand. Of course we can stay just friends. It's fine."

When I got home that night I cried on my bed and poured out my heart to God. "I thought he was 'the one', Lord? At least I thought that's what you were saying. So why did you let me fall in love with him if you knew this was going to happen?"

In reply I 'heard' (internally, not audibly with my ears, but just as clearly) three words: "*Just be patient.*"

In that moment I was convinced that God did have a plan that involved Mike and me together, and with those three words it felt like a blanket of peace settled on my heart and I went to sleep.

I returned to college that weekend and amazingly thought no more about Mike. The command – or rather, blessing – to 'be patient' seemed to have empowered me with the patience that I badly needed. I genuinely, miraculously, forgot about the relationship I was hoping for.

Months later, when I came home for the Christmas holidays, I still had peace about having Mike as a friend, and gladly went to hang out with him again. But as we sat chatting in his flat, he seemed a bit uncomfortable, like he was working himself up to something.

Finally, he took a deep breath. "I need to say sorry."

"Okay," I said, wondering what he meant, "You can say whatever you feel you need to," I said, smiling gently at him.

"I'm sorry for the way I treated you before I left," he said, looking into my eyes.

I had to think hard to remember, as I truly wasn't carrying any hurt. "Please don't worry," I said, trying to put him at ease. I didn't have any problem forgiving him at all.

But he still seemed uneasy, stumbling over his words as he tried to say something else. Eventually he stopped to take a breath, and for a moment the silence fell between us as I waited for him to gather his thoughts.

Then he simply blurted out, "Will you go out with me?"

For a split second I just stared at him. It was completely unexpected: a romantic relationship with Mike was simply not on my radar. I was so shocked that I swore!

It was so out of character for me that he looked taken aback. "No pressure, though," he said quickly. "You don't have to."

But by this point I had regained my equilibrium. I smiled at him. "Yes," I said, nodding firmly. "Yes, of course. I'd love to!"

From that point on it was settled: we were a couple. I later found out that Mike had been deliberating over whether to ask me out at that point or to just cut to the chase and ask me to marry him. I'm glad he opted for the former! I really don't think I would have coped with a proposal at that point. But when he did pop the question just over a year later, I was fully ready and said "yes" without hesitation (or swearing)!

Life was about to throw a curveball before we got to that point, though…

My dreams for my future husband appeared to be crushed…

BUT GOD gave me the patience I needed to wait!

CHAPTER 6

Dealing with Failure

While I was still in my third year at college, my love-life with Mike was now blossoming, but academically I was failing, big time. The work was challenging, but more crucially my internal issues were now sabotaging my studies.

On one hand I was surrounded by new friends, had people helping me to grow spiritually, and was learning about the subjects I loved, but on the other hand I had residual rejection issues and a chronic lack of confidence that nobody around me would have believed. If impostor syndrome had been acknowledged in those days, I would have been its poster girl. Everything around me seemed to be going well but I felt utterly out of control, confused, and, as always, somehow to blame. I had bouts of depression and anorexia, and by the third year was so out of my depth that it felt like I was drowning in defeat.

Teaching practice was now well under way, and although I loved the daily interaction with the children, the recently established National Curriculum was proving to be a stumbling block. I believed in the ideals that teaching was about sparking interest in a child and inspiring them to go on their own journey of discovery, helping them to grow and seeing them reach their potential. But what I was being trained in felt more like an endless paperwork pile of set lesson plans, attainment targets and rigid assessments that left no space for organic development or a tailored approach. My passion rapidly disappeared, to be replaced by disillusionment.

My dream was crumbling before my eyes, and I could only imagine that it was my fault. The very career I had spent my whole life longing for – the only gift or even calling that I felt I had – was turning into a nightmare. My dislike of the National Curriculum, combined with my collapsing self-belief, convinced me that I simply couldn't do it – not like they wanted me to. And the thing that really cemented my failure was my paralysing inability to ask for help. As my internal confusion became darker, it felt as though my new friends were rejecting me, just as peers had in the past, and I did not know how to approach teachers without admitting I had failed or simply wasn't good enough.

So now, in my third year of teacher training college, that weakness was about to put an end to the only career I had ever wanted.

I didn't ask for help; I just winged it – teaching the kids (which I was good at) but without the seemingly soulless but mandatory lesson plans. When the school where I was training discovered my lack of written preparation, the head – as kindly as she could – suggested I talk to the college about whether I was really suited for the job.

By the time I got to the college meeting it was a done deal in my mind. I don't think the college staff would have given up on me so quickly, but I had already been living with this crushing sense of failure for months, if not my entire life. If I had been able to articulate any of this, maybe they would have been able to steer me in the right direction, but all I could see was that I had failed, and I couldn't get out of there fast enough. I called Mike and asked him to pick me up, and I packed my bags. The college was immediately and firmly assigned to my past, but the sense of failure stayed with me.

There were twin demons that haunted me as a result – two overwhelming voices of condemnation that I could not escape. One insisted I had ruined my chances of ever doing the one thing God had called me to do. And the other taunted me with rejection: how could he love me now I had failed him?

The first issue took many years to fully deal with, but the second was – thankfully – swiftly addressed, through many people who God moved through to demonstrate his unconditional love: firstly, Mike, who drove me home from college while I cried the whole way. He was simply there for me, with no judgement.

Secondly, my parents, who welcomed me home again without a word of criticism. They saw my pain and just provided me with a place of refuge once more: no awkward questions, no comments about what it had cost them, no strings attached. Just love.

Thirdly, my church family, who refused to let shame and

condemnation take over completely. Within days of my being home, my lovely friend and house group leader announced that there was a ladies' event that weekend and she was taking me. I wasn't interested, but I didn't have the energy to refuse, so when she turned up that morning, I meekly went with her. I honestly can't remember what the minister shared, but it wasn't as important as what happened at the end – something that would confront me with my recent past...

In my days at Oxford, the church I attended on Sunday mornings had an in-house prophet who regularly gave out words of knowledge[6] from the front to seemingly random people in the congregation. It was intriguing and exciting, and every Sunday I hoped he would get a word from God for me – as if him doing so would somehow validate me as important to God. He never had, though, so when I turned up to the ladies' meeting that morning to see him on the front row with the other ministers, I felt my already downcast heart plummet even further. I had forgotten that the Oxford church was from the same group of churches as my own home church. It was not a pleasant surprise. Here was someone whom I associated with the place of my biggest failure, and whom, in my state of self-pity, I now found myself resenting for never having given me a 'special' word. So I sat through the meeting, unable to stand or sing for the first time in my life, just glaring at him and silently telling God I was not interested. "Don't you dare even think about giving me one of your so-called words," I found myself muttering under my breath (Yep, I was in a bad way).

---

[6] *words of knowledge* – the Holy Spirit-given supernatural ability to tell a fact, circumstance or past event that could not otherwise be known, usually in order to help someone receive God's blessing

The time came for this poor man of God to stand and pronounce his words, and although his eyes passed over me a couple of times, I was greatly relieved when he finished without pointing me out. It had been as much as I could do to allow myself to be taken to a 'God-meeting'; I really couldn't face having everyone look at me while he spoke some nice generic blessings that I felt would have surely been far removed from the pain and failure of my life.

As the meeting ended, I was ready to leave. Nothing had helped, and I didn't know why I had bothered, although I was grateful for the church ladies who had taken me, sat with me, and made sure I knew I was not alone. But then, out of the corner of my eye I saw the prophet approach and pull up a chair next to me and my friend. I was trapped between them. Clearly my glaring hadn't completely put him off. I was grateful at least that he had approached me privately rather than in front of everyone, but my attitude was awful. I just waited for him to spout what I thought would surely be irrelevant niceties, so I could get it over with and leave as quickly as possible.

He started to speak about how I was one of God's precious diamonds: a greatly treasured gem. I now wish I could remember the rest, but in my foolishness, I had already written him off, deciding that it was the sort of thing that he could tell anyone and therefore wasn't worth listening to.

But then he shifted tack. He seemed to be trying to find a way to say something that was puzzling him, as if he didn't quite understand what it could mean. After a few uncomfortable moments, eventually he blurted out, "God wants you to know that your education is very important to him."

Well, he had my attention now! Regretfully I can't remember anything he said after that either, but that was enough. It utterly pierced through my crushing sense of failure and released hope that God was surely there, speaking directly to me. He saw me and was with me – still loving, still inviting me to consider a future with him! He loved me enough to work through a man who I knew gave messages from God, but who related to my place of greatest failure; to speak through him of his love for me and give me hope for the future. Where once I had idly fancied being validated as important enough to be noticed by God, now he knew I really *needed* it. And he met me right where I needed him most.

The prophecy I received gave me the courage to apply to a college closer to home a year later, just after Mike and I were married, and I completed my degree there. Not as a teaching degree – it was converted to a BA (hons) in English – but it was important nonetheless, because it was like a memorial between God and me that even when I felt I failed him, he would never fail me. He was still – and always would be – my friend.

My inadequacy had led to the worst failure I could have imagined…
BUT GOD held on to me!

CHAPTER 7

Unsatisfied

In 1993, Mike and I were married at the old church where I had attended Sunday School as a child, with all our family and friends around us. We held the reception in the town hall where our own church family met. The service was a truly joyful occasion, with the reverend commenting that he'd never seen a bride giggling as she made her way down the aisle (it was a whispered "ooh, very chipper!" from my grandmother as I walked past her that set me off). Our videographer also commented that it was the happiest – and longest – wedding that he'd filmed: a truly joyful day.

After we cleared all the 'just married' paraphernalia obstructing the view out of the windscreen in our car, we made our way onto the M5 to head for Cornwall. I clearly remember a few things from that drive. Firstly, as we chatted comfortably on our journey south, I kept catching a glimpse of my wedding ring and joyfully exclaiming, "We're married!" as I looked forward to a lifetime of sleepovers with my best friend. It was so natural being together that I kept forgetting and then remembering excitedly all over again. However, at some point during our journey we ended up arguing! I'm sure it was over something very trivial, but it seemed to me like a bad omen and I was devastated, my childish fairy tale fantasies of 'happily ever after' immediately shattered. But the disappointment didn't last long, as shortly afterwards we saw a beautiful bright rainbow... and then another... and then another! Three rainbows in succession were a much better omen and I felt God was saying that even though we had not been promised a fairy tale ending, and that the storms of life may come, he was with us still and had promised to not let us be destroyed.

And so, we began married life. Mike had a job in Cheltenham where I was also now going to college to finish my degree, so we were able to travel together most days. We had scraped together to buy a modest ex-council house with horribly dated carpets and wallpaper, and a slightly musty smell from being empty a long time. But it also had a huge front room, three bedrooms and a generous, somewhat unkempt garden. We had very little by way of furniture. Mike brought a sofa from his flat that had been rescued by a friend when she saw it being thrown out elsewhere, and his single bed for our spare room. For our first marital bed we slept on a bed-settee that consisted of two painfully narrow ancient mattresses balanced on two equally narrow metal frames with a hard ridge between them. My grandparents bought a washing machine for us, and my parents donated – among other things – the old Narnia-esque wardrobe from my childhood. Our sparsely furnished house was shared with a succession of pet gerbils who multiplied uncontrollably and occasionally caused havoc by escaping and getting everywhere they shouldn't.

The group of young singles who we were friends with at church had become a group of young couples, including my sister and her fiancé. As Mike and I were the first to get married, our house became the hangout for lots of fun socials, including *Pictionary* tournaments that went down in legend among us. But it wasn't just silly games that we enjoyed together – we also met up as a church group for training. We took tests to reveal our spiritual gifts (mine came out as equal Servant and Prophet, which our pastor didn't know what to do with), and we studied the Bible and prayed for each other.

It was at about this time that the older children in our church youth group started to learn how to receive and give words of knowledge from God, like the ones given by the prophet from Oxford. I looked at these young ones and thought, "Well, if they can do it, why can't I?" The gifts of the Holy Spirit that had always seemed the exclusive domain of important church leaders suddenly became something that were available to anybody, even me. I asked God to speak to me so I could bless other people, and he did. It was never in an audible (to human ears) voice, but over time I began receiving impressions, thoughts that weren't my own, and mental images. These 'words' seemed to be random, occasional gifts, but were always exciting to receive!

My degree course finished, and I graduated in 1994, after which I got a job as a special support assistant, helping children with special educational needs in local schools. It took a lot of courage to go back into an educational setting, and I had to overcome an ever-present niggling sense that I didn't belong, but I wasn't responsible for lesson plans or written assessments, and I just got to do what I enjoyed the most in helping kids to learn, so I loved it. The work didn't last, though – they were only temporary placements, so when they dried up, I went back to work for a family whom I had worked with in the year before I got married, as a part-time mother's help. They were a lovely Christian family – I was always happiest when surrounded by children – and Mike and I felt settled, for a while at least.

I can't say exactly when it started, but at some point during those years I started feeling really restless. God was still my friend – there was no problem there. I was growing in faith, singing on the worship team, being discipled[7] by some truly godly people, and able to use some of the gifts of the Spirit. But I was also growing very dissatisfied. This spiritual growth seemed encouraging, but as I read my Bible and saw again how radical Jesus was: raising the dead, healing the sick, casting out demons – and how his first disciples followed in his footsteps, I began to question why that wasn't happening around me. I felt like a fraud in comparison. But this time it wasn't like the old shame-based impostor syndrome – it felt like a God-inspired hunger for more of his reality in my life. And it became like an itch that wouldn't go away. Nothing I could do eased it. I prayed, and prayed some more, but nothing seemed to

---

[7] *Discipled* – being encouraged to follow and apply Jesus Christ's teachings more closely, by someone more mature and experienced in their Christian relationship with God

change. I asked anyone and everyone to pray for me, because I just knew there was more to Christianity than what I was experiencing. My friends and leaders did pray for me, but still the dissatisfaction persisted, and it got to the point where I'm sure they wished I would just calm down and stop making a big deal out of nothing, because as far as they were concerned, I was already on the right track to spiritual maturity. Yet the dissatisfaction remained, and I did not know what to do about it.

One day in church a notice was read out that there were some Christians coming to our town to do a mission outreach. They were coming from over a hundred miles away, so needed places to stay, and did anyone have any spare beds/rooms that they could use? It makes me smile to think of our basic little ex-council house now, but at the time we were young and naïve, and just loved hosting people, so we quickly volunteered to have as many people as could fit in our two spare rooms (never mind that we only had one single spare bed!)

The people who came to stay were called Chris and Mark. They and their team were Christians like we had never met before: they prayed bold prayers, cast out demons, and healed the sick – maybe not on the same scale as Jesus, but still with a level of faith that I had never experienced – and I loved it! At one point I even received instant healing myself. It happened in a meeting where they were training people to pray with those who wanted to be born again during the mission. During the meeting I started to experience a severe pain in my head and face – I wasn't sure if it was toothache or neuralgia, but I just wanted to get home to get some painkillers, and rest. The meeting finished soon after and I stood up to leave. When

Mark (who was leading the meeting) saw me he asked if I was OK as I looked so pale. I said I was in pain and going home, and he promptly offered to pray. I gladly agreed, so he immediately took my face in his hands and commanded the pain to leave... and it went! Instantly! It was such a relief. I grinned and thanked him and got my coat. He gave me a hug and suggested I go home to rest, but I promptly told him I was doing no such thing – I was healed, and I was going shopping!

I realised these people lived their lives according to the Bible and I loved how they refused to compromise on it. They were full of life and faith, and I loved it. They taught us, prayed for us, and had many meals with us – and by the time the mission came to an end, with many people in Stroud healed and born again as a result, I was changed for good. After the last meeting I couldn't speak; I was overcome with tears – but it wasn't because I was sad that it was over and our new friends were going – it was because I was so grateful that God had answered my prayers for more, and I knew I would never be the same.

Little did I know just how significant this time would prove to be, as our lives were about to undergo even greater change...

I didn't know what I wanted, or how to get it...
BUT GOD knew, and He satisfied every longing!

CHAPTER 8

Uncomfortable

Over the months that followed the mission, we were delighted to discover that our new friendships were not just temporary. Our friends came back regularly to minister in the area, and each time they stayed with Mike and me, and encouraged us more in our faith. Sometimes we visited them too. All in all, over the year that followed the mission there was not a month that went by without us seeing Chris or Mark, either in our hometown or one of theirs. Exposed to a rich new stream of faith, my relationship with God was growing rapidly. I developed a habit of starting my mornings praying and reading the Bible, which helped me enormously in getting to know God even better, and always got my days off to a positive start.

Unfortunately, this was not without problems. For example,

one of the Bible studies that we were given was about healing. I remembered the prophecy that had been given to me as a student about a healing ministry and loved how it seemed to tie in with what I was now seeing. I didn't just want to take any one person's word for it though – I wanted to know what the Bible said. So I studied it for myself, and quickly discovered in the New Testament that every person who came to Jesus for healing went away healed. To my mind, if the Bible said it, then it was true, and I felt that if we were failing to receive healing, it wasn't because the Bible was untrue, but had to be due to human misunderstanding. I was very new to this kind of teaching and was probably very clumsy in expressing my faith for healing, as it caused quite some upset in our church. Some loved it and were healed when we prayed – while others felt we were causing upset if people did not get healed. Our wonderful leaders did not tell us to stop praying, but they did advise us to be more tactful in our approach.

There was another time when a group of us (including some young believers who had been born again during the mission) met up to pray and worship. During the worship one of the new believers started to wail strangely and it became apparent that a demon was involved. I really did not know what I was doing – I knew this happened in Jesus' day, and had heard that it still happened today, but felt completely out of my depth. So, I did the only thing I felt I could do, and kept worshipping Jesus and praying for her, until the demon left. There was no formula – the group of us were just trying to follow the Holy Spirit's leading – but by the end she was at peace, convinced that it had gone, so we celebrated with her.

However, the next Sunday we became aware of quite a stir

as some in the church started murmuring and complaining that we should not have done this as we weren't qualified to cast out demons. They were right that we hadn't received any training in that area and did not know what we were doing, and so even though we hadn't pursued it intentionally, we were concerned that we had accidentally done wrong and went to ask our pastor about it. He seemed slightly bemused at everything going on, but in his wisdom, he merely commented that as far as he was aware they didn't hand out badges that allowed only certain people to cast out demons. So we felt released from having done wrong.

Our home church was becoming quite uncomfortable by now, though, and we were starting to feel that if we stayed, we could cause a church split between those who welcomed the direction God was leading us in and those who resisted. We loved our church family – we didn't want to bring division. It felt like the feathers were being plucked out of our once cosy nest – that we no longer belonged there. So, Mike and I prayed about it, together and individually, to ask God if he was calling us somewhere else. I felt that the two most likely places were either Chris's hometown or Mark's. We had been to both places several times by now and loved all the people, so I picked one, and said to God, "Are you calling us to be a part of Chris's church?"

Immediately I felt a barrier inside – it was like a divine "No" resounding throughout me, shutting down that train of thought – and that was that. I was disappointed, but at least there was a second, also appealing option. This time I asked God rather nervously if he was calling us to Ely (Mark's hometown), hoping I wasn't about to be shut down again.

But it was like an internal door opened, right in that moment. I saw a succession of mental pictures of us working with Mark and his wife Sandra, ministering, serving, and growing, on a new adventure. That was all I needed to know – it was settled in me. But I promptly asked God to tell Mike himself: I was growing more confident in my ability to discern God's leading, but this seemed a huge risk to take if I was wrong. Also, I did not want our decision to depend on my ability (or lack of) to persuade Mike.

A while later Mike and I had a visit from Mark. We had a good catch-up chat, then he said he had a proposition for us. He explained that he and Sandra had been praying for a couple to come and join them in their ministry, to work alongside them and support them in the practical day-to-day running of things. They had felt called to hold a conference and it had all been booked, but they had received a prophecy that they wouldn't have to do it alone – God was going to join them with a couple of 'armour-bearers'[8] who would move to support them and release the ministry to grow. "We prayed about it," he said, "and we both feel that God might be saying this could be you two. So... what do you think?"

I waited for Mike to speak, as I already knew what I thought. Mike was smiling. "Well... God's actually just shown me something. It's simple, but I'm convinced." He went on to explain. The place where we lived at the time was a little place called Ebley. We used to play a game like the TV game show *Catchphrase*, where a phrase was hidden inside a word puzzle

---

[8] *armour-bearer* – In the Bible an armour-bearer was an assistant who carried their leader's armour, and in modern times this usually translates as a close, trusted assistant who deals with the practical running of ministry as well as supporting spiritually, through prayer.

or picture – and God had revealed to Mike that 'Ebley' was a play on words for "Be in Ely".

Mark looked bemused but delighted, and turned to me – would I also be convinced by this simple idea? He seemed shocked to discover I was just sitting there grinning. The whole time they had been talking I had been inwardly laughing with joy. I had already heard God – and we were moving to Ely!

We felt out of place, no longer comfortable and at home...
BUT GOD had a new adventure planned for us.

CHAPTER 9

A New Adventure

That move to Ely was the most exciting time. We were young and naïve enough to believe we could change the world. It was a real wrench to leave my family behind, but I believed God had a good plan and he had promised to be with us, so we went, relying on him to help us as we said 'goodbye'.

Finding a house was the first challenge. We travelled to Ely for a day to look around a few rental properties, but they were all rough: old, damp and unloved. None of them seemed right. Then, just as we were finishing up at the last place, feeling discouraged and dejected, the letting agent mentioned there was one more that was just about to come onto their books, and did we want to have a look? Well of course we did! He went to collect the keys and took us to the house in question.

But then we hit a snag. The keys to the back door didn't work. He tried everything he could think of, but the door would not budge. By now I was getting fed up with the barriers that seemed to be trying to prevent our obeying God, so I started praying under my breath for the door to open. The agent turned to us to apologise that we couldn't see inside after all and gave it a final half-hearted shove of regret... at which point it flew open! We were in, and immediately knew we had found our home – it was up-to-date and clean *and* it was big enough to share with others, which meant we'd be able to cover the rent when we moved in a few weeks later.

Neither of us had a paying job to go to – Mark and Sandra had been completely open with us and explained they had no money to offer us, as they were living by faith for their own family – so if we went, we would have to trust God to provide. We knew God had called us so we had no doubt he would deal with the costs incurred in obeying. It wasn't long after we moved in that we found our first lodger from our new church... and then another. For two people who loved being around others, it was such a blessing to have people live with us. Not that there weren't challenges – of course there were. But generally we were grateful to be getting to know our new church family, and to be living in a decent home. With no earnings we really were reliant on God for everything. We had a small income coming in from our old house in Ebley that we were renting out, but it only covered that mortgage and a bit of our rent.

Yet after a while we had so many experiences of God supernaturally providing food and/or money that it became sort of normal – whether it was an anonymous food parcel left on our doorstep, perfectly timed gifts, or a bank balance that was impossibly in the black. It was such a difficult path to walk, but it stretched our faith and God met us there.

Our new church leaders were people of strong faith who were uncompromising in trusting God to heal the sick, provide financially, and work other miracles. And alongside this strong faith they ran courses called 'Family Life Skills' for emotional wellbeing. Mike and I joined right away, and it was such a gift to us, giving us the emotional tools to understand ourselves better – why certain things triggered negative responses internally, and how to deal with it. As both of us still had residual issues in our lives it was a very healing process. I am so thankful to God for that season of training, both emotionally and in matters of faith.

There was one more course that they ran that also changed my life, and that was on hearing the voice of God[9]. For the first time someone sat me down and took me through a series of teaching and practical exercises around hearing God's voice – still not audibly, the way we hear people talking in soundwaves, but in an internal way, through thoughts, feelings, and mental images. I started keeping a journal where I wrote down the things that I felt God might be saying in my prayer times and shared those words with trusted leaders who helped me hone the ability to 'hear' further. From that point on my prayer times gradually became something less formal and more like simply hanging out, having two-way chats with God, my friend. I still struggled at times with all the usual distractions and feelings of not being good enough and so on. But learning to discern God's voice more was absolutely one of

[9] *Communion with God* by Mark & Patti Virkler

the best gifts I've been given to help me in my relationship with him.

Pretty soon Mark, Mike and I were travelling around the country most weekends, ministering in various conferences and churches. And even though we were travelling to bless others, we were often blessed in return, like the time we visited quite a poor little town in South Wales. After the meeting, as people milled around chatting, I spotted a young family and felt a strong sense that the daughter had a call on her life to be actively engaged in worship, particularly in dance. I approached the mum and told her what I felt, and both she and the girl got excited. "This is her absolute dream!" the mum said, and then she started sharing with me about her older son who was also there but loitering near the back of the room, reluctant to join in. She told me that he had just failed in a certain area and was very discouraged, wondering if he had ruined his chance for God to work through him.

Instantly I was flooded with thanks for God's kindness in bringing this lad and me to this point. I realised in that moment how God had set me free from the curse of failure that I thought was over my life since dropping out of college – and that although I once thought I had ruined my chance of fulfilling his call on my life, I was now living the most exciting and fulfilling adventure with him that I could have imagined! And of course, I was able to tell the young man, and pray with the family for each of them to walk in the unique plans and adventures that God had in store for them.

Then there was a meeting in Suffolk when Mark was praying for many people in the congregation. I was praying at one side when I became aware of a voice (again, not an audible one, but an internal impression) saying "I want you". At first I thought it was a loving voice, affirming God's desire for my friendship, but as I continued worshipping, I started to feel uneasy, like there was something oppressive around me that did not want me to be free. Even though we were there to serve the church, I felt I needed to receive prayer for myself, so after the congregation had been prayed for I asked Mark and he readily agreed, praying for the hostile presence to leave. That evening I felt the peaceful presence of God fill me again, which was beautiful and a huge relief. But it was only in the days, weeks and months that followed that I realised the shame, rejection, and at times depression, that I had struggled with for most of my life was now gone. I would still have problems to deal with, of course, but even though doubt and difficult circumstances would arise from time to time, these feelings were no longer part of me. I was free.

I had been held back, haunted by things from my past...
BUT GOD set me free!

CHAPTER 10

The Barren Years

We lived in and around Ely for six years. Sharing our house with a succession of lodgers was challenging at times, and the busy ministry schedule could be exhausting. But we made friends there who are among our closest friends still, we grew as people immeasurably, and overall it really felt like a great adventure.

I do think it's important to recognise the joy of those years. Because while the adventure was unfolding and we were seeing God bless many people, there was one area that meant those years in Ely were also some of the most painful of my life.

In the year before we left Ebley, Mike and I had decided we were ready to start a family. We'd been married a couple of years, and felt it was as good a time as any to get started on our brood. We'd been given many prophecies about having a large family and me being a 'Mum to many', and we were excited for the first baby or two to arrive. But after a few months it didn't happen, and after several more months we were rather disheartened. I remembered a time when I had naively told God, "I wouldn't mind if we are unable to have kids so that you can do a miracle in us." But I pushed it to the back of my mind and carried on trying, sure that our blessings couldn't be far away. The excitement of moving to Ely and becoming 'full-time ministers' was a welcome distraction for a time, but after a while Mike and I realised that as we had been trying to conceive for two years, it would probably be wise to talk to our GP. Not that we wanted them to give us a negative diagnosis, but we were inspired by Abraham from the Bible, who 'faced the facts' about his and his wife's infertility, but 'didn't waver in faith'.[10] We decided that we didn't have to be afraid of whatever the doctors might find, because if Abraham's faith could overcome their facts, so could ours.

Our GP referred us to fertility specialists straight away, and we underwent the usual tests. It didn't take them long to find an issue, and they informed us that we were unable to conceive naturally. The specialist said there was a very specialised form of IVF that we might be able to try, but even if we did, the odds were cruelly stacked against us. We said we would consider it, and we went home and prayed.

We were devastated, naturally – alternating between numb and grieving. But somehow underneath it all was that tiny spark of hope from when I had told God I wouldn't mind if he wanted to give us miracle children, and from the example of

---

[10] Romans 4:19

Abraham and Sarah's faith. Amidst all the pain and difficulty of that season, it felt like an opportunity for him to show his power.

I wasn't sure about IVF. I knew it to be a lifeline for many childless couples, and the urge to do whatever it took to conceive was intense – but I had three real concerns on top of wondering whether or not it would even work. Firstly, the cost – we simply did not have thousands of pounds to spare. Secondly, the stress – fertility treatment is renowned for putting couples under enormous pressure. Our desire for a family was already a huge deal in our lives; would we handle it taking over completely? And lastly – really my biggest concern – how ethical it was. So, I prayed. I poured out my heart to God and admitted that whatever path we took, I knew it was going to require significant faith – whether faith to conceive without medical intervention, or faith for God to provide everything we needed for the IVF to be a complete success, with no embryos left over. I told God that I was ready to follow whichever route he wanted, to have the children he had promised, if he would just lead us to his best plan for us. Immediately I heard his words in my heart: *"I'm going to do it supernaturally."*

I told Mike that I felt we weren't supposed to take the IVF route and he agreed. So we set our faith to trust God that however impossible it was, he was going to give us children supernaturally. The years that followed would seriously test that faith.

The irony wasn't lost on me of being involved in a faith ministry, travelling around the country, speaking hope to people, and seeing them receive their miracles, while every month receiving symptoms that shouted "God's not coming through for us." It was at times unbearably painful. Any woman who has longed for a baby will know how those hormones take over your life and make it hard to focus on anything else, and I wasn't just hormonal! I was also clinging to a single, six-word promise that I believed I had heard, that God would give us babies supernaturally. Every month felt like a battle of faith versus discouragement, and every monthly period made me feel like I had failed again, that maybe God wasn't listening, and the enemy had won.

We told Mark and Sandra and they immediately agreed with us in faith that God would provide our miracle. We told our other friends and pastors in Ely, knowing that they would agree with our prayers – and they did. We also told Chris and his wife, as well as their pastor who by now was also a friend, having seen us at many conferences. They all agreed to pray with and for us, trusting that God would keep his promise. There were times when we needed to escape the pressures at home in Ely and would go to visit them for some breathing space – and invariably, as soon as their pastor saw me, he would give me a big grin and call out "Hello, pregnant!", declaring his faith and encouraging our faith too. I am so thankful for the people of faith that God surrounded us with.

We found out years later that there were many other people around us who found out about our struggles and thought we were completely deluded: they just felt sorry for us, doubting that we would ever conceive. I don't blame them: we were barren for many years, which was an awfully long time to keep hoping. I'm just grateful that we were oblivious to their unbelief at the time.

During the barren years we seemed to attract people who

would prophesy over us about our promised babies. Initially it was really encouraging to hear people reaffirming the promise we felt God had given us for children. But the problem came when those prophesying didn't stop with the promise but started to predict specific time frames. The first time, we were in a prayer group with a sweet little old lady who said, "God's going to give you a baby by this time next month, and it's because he loves you so much." I was so excited! I told our home group and started planning the nursery, setting my heart on her words without asking God for his confirmation. It only took a couple of weeks to discover that we were *not* pregnant, and I was devastated. I'd had a late cycle a few times and got my hopes up a little, but not like this. According to her 'prophecy', God was giving me a baby that month because he loved me... so did this lack of babies mean he *didn't* love me? Thankfully I had the sense – albeit belatedly – to ask God about it. He showed me that although she had sensed his promise accurately, she had also felt his compassion and misinterpreted it, applying what she – or I – *wanted* to be true. She wanted to make me feel better but ultimately it made things harder.

Sadly, she wasn't the only one. In time, we had so many people predicting specific dates over us that always turned out to be wrong, that in the end I prayed and asked God to stop those dodgy prophecies. He told me he wouldn't send any prophecies involving specific dates, so that if anyone, whoever they were, prophesied a set timeline over me for when our babies would arrive, I would now know it wasn't from him. With that established, the false prophecies stopped coming, and I was able to focus back on trusting God for his perfect but unknown timing.

Whether battling false prophecies or just the doubts that rose within myself over this prolonged season, those barren years were marked with painful disappointment, the overwhelming longing of my empty arms, and the regular temptation to sink into hopelessness with every month that passed, still not pregnant.

When I felt strong enough, I would copy out all the promises from the Bible to do with barrenness and fruitfulness; I would pray, speaking out my trust in God; and I would read books on miracles (especially of the baby-conceiving kind). Then, when it got too overwhelming, I would cry and pour out my broken heart to God: "I can't do this any more," I would sob to him. "It's too hard, trying to build my faith and keep trusting in your promises." I would confess that I wasn't strong enough to keep believing – the pain was too great, and I was too weak. And in those times of hot cascading tears I would feel a sense of his presence, as if his arms were around me, his peace settling over me. "I need a break," I would say. "I don't have it in me to keep praying, confessing, and waiting in hope."

And then I would lay it all down and try to stop thinking about it, distracting myself with ministry work, just trusting in his love to carry me. After a week or two of resting from the fight of faith, I would start to hear his voice whispering hope to my heart again, reminding me of his promises and his faithfulness, and encouraging me to start praying and hoping again.

I was tempted to let go of God's promises because of the pain and cost involved...
BUT GOD never let go of me!

63

CHAPTER 11

Promise Fulfilled

In 2000 things were starting to change in Ely. Mark and Sandra and Mike and I were feeling restless. Itinerant ministry was exciting, but we were all starting to feel hungry for something more long-term than sporadic visits – something where we could really invest in people's growth. It was the beginning of a desire to start a church. We were all praying and asking God to direct us, when we received a letter containing an urgent prayer request from someone in Stevenage. It was a place where we already knew a few people who supported the ministry but where they didn't feel there was a church that would really help them grow in faith. That letter turned out to be a pivotal point in God calling us, as it wasn't much longer before Mark and Sandra sat us down and said they felt called to move to Stevenage to plant a church. They did not place any demands on Mike and me, just suggested we pray and see what God was saying. We dutifully did so, but I already knew – we were called there too. God had called us to serve Mark and Sandra as armour-bearers, so in my mind it didn't matter where they lived – we were committed to serving them anywhere. But Mike and I had also felt the call specifically to Stevenage for ourselves – we knew God had a purpose for us there too; a purpose not just to fulfil someone else's vision.

As the four of us started telling others of our vision there was a mixed response. Some people were very positive, and we received some encouraging prophecies. Other people were less heartening, and we received more than one comment along the lines of "Stevenage? THAT wilderness?" But we weren't deterred – we knew God had called us. And a couple of friends in Stevenage felt it too, so they opened their home to us, and we all started meeting there together for prayer, asking God to show us the next steps.

That small group grew rapidly, and we quickly needed a bigger place to meet. We found an old school that had plenty of room for offices as well as somewhere to gather on Sunday mornings. By February 2001 Mike and I had bought a house in Stevenage and moved there, while Mark and Sandra were in the process of selling theirs.

Not long after that, Mike and I were both feeling worn out. We put it down to the busy-ness of ministry and the stresses involved in buying a house, and prayed for a holiday. Having just moved house we didn't have much money left, but God provided a beautiful holiday and off we went, looking forward to a much-needed chance to rest. With all our previous holidays, we had always returned home recharged and ready to get back into the swing of things. But as we approached the end of this holiday, I found I wasn't as refreshed and looking forward to going home as usual. In fact, I was dreading it. Not because of church or ministry – that was still going well – but it had all become overshadowed by the immense and overwhelming pain of still not having children. After so many years of praying and standing in faith since we first pinned our hopes on God's promise, I felt I had truly come to the end of my ability to keep fighting. I was now so reluctant to come home that I realised I just couldn't carry on without children. I hadn't given up on God's promise to give us supernatural babies, but the physical ache to hold a child in my arms, peg little clothes out on the washing line to dry, and give goodnight kisses to sleepyheads had become genuinely unbearable. I simply HAD to have children in my home and could not go without any longer. So, Mike and I talked and agreed that when we got back, we would commence the process to become foster parents while waiting for our own babies. It gave me something positive to focus on, and when we got home, we arranged a visit from a social worker and signed up to a training course.

At church, the Sunday morning meetings continued to grow, but it was the smaller mid-week prayer meetings that I remember as being most powerful in terms of receiving vision and answers to prayer. There was a particular prayer meeting that I will never forget. We were praying for Stevenage and the church, when God took me to a verse that I think was Isaiah 41:18 or a similar verse along the lines of him turning the barren wilderness (i.e. Stevenage) into a rich and fertile place.

We had been given several similar verses before, but this time was different, because after God whispered that verse to my heart, he told me that to prove it, my barren womb was now going to receive life: I was going to conceive and have a baby!

At that point we had been trying and failing to conceive for six-and-a-half years. Since my deal with God about the false prophecies, nobody else had brought up the subject – but even having God tell me himself was not easy to receive. I promptly told him it was not a fair thing to say, and I 'shelved' it, putting it to the back of my mind.

Shortly after that we had our young niece and nephew to stay, giving me chance to indulge my maternal instincts right away. We excitedly welcomed our young relatives for a few days of fun and distraction, but the problem was, those 'few fun days' took their toll more than I expected! At one point I took them to a local park, and as I sat on the picnic blanket under a tree watching them explore the playground, I was overwhelmed by weariness. I just wanted to lie down and take a nap, which was not like me at all. Of course I didn't – I was responsible for small people after all – but the exhaustion was not a good sign. It crossed my mind to wonder if I might be pregnant at last – by now I knew every tiny sign and symptom of pregnancy by heart – but I quickly dismissed the idea. I was fed up with getting excited at every slight possible hint and I concluded that it was more likely glandular fever!

As I tried to muster the energy to get up, I felt as if I could hear God chuckle, and then tease me joyfully: "*You were always going to have pregnancy symptoms that turned out to be true one day!*" But although I was usually confident in being able to hear God's voice by now, my self-protection mechanisms kicked in. I may have been living in faith that we would conceive *one day*, but I was unable to connect with the faith for it to be *today*, and steadfastly refused to let myself get my hopes up for the promise to arrive there and then.

I dragged myself off the blanket and trailed around the park after the children, revelling in the sound of their laughter and distracting myself from how exhausted I was. The next day my brother and sister-in-law came to pick the children up. My sister-in-law was very concerned about how tired I looked and worried that the children had been a handful, but I assured her they hadn't – they were a total delight! We were sad to see them go, but once they had left, I wanted to do one thing before heading for a nap. I found a pregnancy test from the small stash that we always had in those days, and dutifully peed on it. Then I put it on the toilet cistern behind me, not daring to look until the full five minutes were up – still trying not to allow myself to hope.

Finally, I stood up and prepared myself for the inevitable sense of disappointment that had always accompanied previous tests. No matter how much I told myself not to get my hopes up, there was always a tiny part of me that wouldn't co-operate and was subsequently always crushed when the test showed no pregnancy.

I picked the test up, stared at it, and then put it down again. I looked at the instruction sheet, and then picked up the test again. But what I was seeing didn't make sense to somebody who was expecting a negative result. I stared at it again and read the instructions again, but still didn't quite believe what the two lines were telling me…

So I called out, panicked, for a second opinion. "Mike!"

He came right away – must have heard something in my voice – and I held out the test stick to show him, the beautiful truth only just starting to break through my denial. He was a lot faster to comprehend and started celebrating right away.

The celebrations continued for days, if not weeks and months. Everyone we told rejoiced with us – even the social worker who generously congratulated us when we had to call to put our fostering plans on hold. And we received so many bouquets of flowers we ran out of vases to hold them! The day we told our church family that we were expecting was a total joy – they were thrilled for us, and for the prophecy that God had given the church through it. And my parents and grandparents, who were already talking about moving in together, decided it wouldn't be much harder buying a house in Stevenage than it was in Stroud, so they started the proceedings to move over to be near their new (great) grandchild. My sister and brother-in-law felt the same, and before long I had the joy of having most of my family living nearby again. It had been so hard to leave them when we moved to Ely, but several years later it felt like God had brought them back to me.

I would say the pregnancy was uneventful, but every symptom, every craving, and every kick was an event to be celebrated. For several weeks I had to leave the kitchen if Mike started cooking onions because the smell turned my stomach. My consumption of bananas and marmite (not at the same time) dramatically increased. When we went to a conference several hours drive away, the journey took longer than planned because of the frequent stops for toilet breaks. And the tiredness! Sometimes I could barely drag myself upstairs to get to bed. But I relished every single moment of it because it was all due to the miracle growing inside me. I particularly loved my doctor and midwife appointments and saw them as a welcome celebration that the thing I had longed for most in the world was now here. The 12-week scan when I set eyes on the first grainy black-and-white images of my precious unborn baby was the most beautiful thing I had ever seen – and when we discovered at twenty weeks that we were having a boy, we could not have been more excited. I absolutely loved my growing bump – even when my baby stretched his legs so far I felt sure a foot would break through my belly! I simply savoured every moment, right up until the last few days when my hormones changed, and I suddenly became Ready-with-a-capital-R for my baby to arrive!

My waters broke in the early hours one morning in spring 2002, just a few days before our due date. Labour wasn't entirely straightforward: it turned out my baby was lying with his back along my back, but eventually he was delivered with the help of forceps. The midwife told me most babies are born facing down to the floor, but ours was born gazing up to the heavens. Even though it had made for a slightly more difficult delivery, I thought that was a lovely image. She passed him up to me and placed him carefully on my chest. As I rested my hand on his precious little body and gazed into the depths of his beautiful eyes gazing back at me, I whispered the loving words I had waited over seven years to say: "Hello, son!"

Our promised baby was here at last.

The doctors said we could not have babies naturally…
BUT GOD gave them to us supernaturally!

CHAPTER 12

The Valley of the Shadow

With a new miracle baby as the absolute joy of our lives, and a rapidly growing church to serve, our lives were now very busy! Those years were such happy times – the pain of the barren years was diminishing in my memory, and my biggest problem as a new (sleep-deprived) mum was trying to make sure I got time with God. My once regular morning prayer time was not at all regular anymore, but I did manage to grab time with him periodically. One day when I was praying, I heard him put a question to my heart: "*Are you ready to go deeper?*" I really had no idea what he meant, but of course I said, "Yes, Lord!" It was always the desire of my heart to know him better – I don't think it's the sort of thing where one ever feels satisfied – so I naturally agreed. Little did I know that I was about to experience the most painful time of my life.

My baby was now a toddler keeping me very busy, but was such a blessing we were keen to keep adding to our family. Technically we were still unable to conceive, but God had promised us multiple babies, and we had living proof that an infertility diagnosis was no barrier to God. Soon we received confirmation that we had another miracle baby on the way. We were thrilled! The new baby was due to be born a few months after Joshua's second birthday, which we felt was a perfect age gap, and we couldn't wait to share the news, which again led to great rejoicing.

At about 11 weeks along, I started 'spotting'; losing small amounts of blood. A call to the GP eased my concerns slightly as he said it was quite normal in many pregnancies, but I was still uneasy. I did my best to rest for the next few days before my 12-week scan when I hoped to be reassured that all was well. That first scan had been such a source of joy last time, I couldn't wait to see my new baby, and focused on that.

The day of the scan I dutifully drank so much water I could barely hold it in, and we laughed nervously in the waiting room as I crossed my legs, trying not to think about using the toilet. In the ultrasound room I chatted excitedly with Mike in anticipation of seeing our new unborn baby for the first time. But within moments all our smiles vanished as the sonographer turned the screen to face us and gently explained that our baby had died in the womb. The placenta had carried on growing, but our baby had not – and all I could see on the screen was a dark gaping space where my baby was supposed to be.

I was numb.

My baby had died.

At some point we were given the option of having a surgical procedure to remove what was referred to as the 'products of conception', or to go home and 'let nature take its course'. We chose the latter, as I simply wasn't ready to accept the brutal end to my pregnancy. And all I wanted was to go home and hold my living, breathing toddler.

So that's what we did. It was a few days before Christmas, and I decided to try to take my mind off things by taking little Joshy to see the Christmas lights in town. I quickly discovered this was a foolish idea. Grief is not something that one can easily switch off. Every person I saw merrily going about their normal everyday life was a reminder that I couldn't just do the same. It's an old cliché, but we only discover the truth of it when we encounter grief for ourselves: it comes as a total and unwelcome shock to discover that life goes on. I was miserably stunned to discover that there were thousands of people out there whose worlds hadn't ended – and it made me feel utterly alien and isolated in my pain. So I went home and stayed home, cocooned with my loved ones as we tried to come to terms with our loss.

A couple of days later I realised 'letting nature take its course' was not necessarily the kinder or more gentle option. The light spotting had turned to a much heavier blood loss. I had picked up a cold, and as I sat in my rocking chair that afternoon trying to watch *White Christmas* with my toddler snuggled into me, I could not stop coughing. Every cough released a fresh flow of blood, and I had to go to the bathroom to clean up every few minutes. After a while we realised it was not stopping and had to seek medical help. We had been given the number for the gynaecological ward, and when we phoned, they asked us to come straight in. My parents came over to babysit, and Mike and I drove through the busy, brightly coloured streets to the hospital.

My abiding memory of Christmas Eve that year is of lying in a side room with medical professionals working inside me to try to stop the bleeding as the last vestiges of my pregnancy inevitably and brutally came to an end, all while the visiting Salvation Army band played *Away in a Manger* to the other patients on the rest of the ward. Mike and I shared a brief ironic smile and prayed that God would stop the bleeding so I could go home and spend Christmas Day with my little boy. Soon after, the bleeding was brought under control and I was released just after midnight on Christmas morning, in plenty of time to get some rest before Joshua woke up to open his presents.

We went to our church Christmas service that morning, tired and sad, but determined to attend. I have always been a Christmas kid at heart – I love all the twinkly lights, joyful carols, gift-giving and so on, and I felt I had a choice: to let the joy of Christmas be robbed from me forever by associating it with pain and loss, or to celebrate it still. Because however sore my heart was, the fact remained that Christmas is a time to celebrate the gift of my friend Jesus. And I was not about to let that joy be robbed from me as well as my unborn baby, however confused or hurt I was. So, although I was too weak from blood-loss to stand, I chose to sing and worship him still, because even in the pain, he was still worth celebrating.

And during the Christmas service that morning, cocooned in the love and sympathy of church friends and family, there were two things that filled me with hope. Firstly, without being orchestrated by anyone, the children in the congregation came to sit with me. One of them told me that she knew my baby had died – it was strangely comforting to hear her blunt acknowledgement of our loss – and then the other children gradually all drew near and simply sat next to and around me for the rest of the service. It was hugely comforting and felt like a precious reminder that God hadn't forgotten his promise: he was still going to surround me with children.

The second thing that impacted me was the sermon. I wasn't very aware of Mark's words, as I was still emotionally mostly numb. But as I sat and enjoyed the comforting presence of my little Josh on my lap and the other children all about me, I suddenly heard one sentence cut through my fuzzy thoughts as Mark quoted a Bible verse where God said 'I will never leave you'[11]

As Mark read the verse aloud, I heard God speak firmly and directly to my heart, saying, "*I will not, WILL NOT,* **WILL NOT** *ever leave you.*"

It felt like I had been holding my breath – that amidst all the emotional pain of losing my baby and the physical ordeal it had been, there had also been an attempt to steal my relationship with God. I realised that subconsciously there had been two questions churning deep inside:

Was it my fault?

Where is God now?

The medical community had been quick to answer the first question by assuring me that it was not because of anything I had done physically, which was some comfort. But the second question was even more important to me, and was the one I

---

[11] Hebrews 13:5

had unknowingly been holding my breath for: where IS God when pain becomes overwhelming, and we seem to be defeated? As Mark preached the sermon that Christmas morning and God spoke the comforting truth of his presence to my heart, I knew I would be OK. He was with me still. He had never left me before; he wouldn't leave me now (and decades later, he still hasn't left me. He's faithful like that).

His assurance of that Christmas would carry me through the season to come. I've been told that some people deal with miscarriage in a far less intense way, but I was totally bereft. It hit me deeply, and I grieved long and hard. My longed-for new baby had died, and I was heartbroken. My toddler was as much a source of blessing as ever – truly a source of comfort – but still I grieved, plunged deep into the valley of the shadow of death. And it was there that I discovered the truth of Psalm 23, for God truly was with me every step of the way.

It took me months, maybe more than a year, to recover emotionally. Most of the time I managed to hold together a semblance of normality, but when the Christmas decorations came down and we had to move into the new year being not pregnant; when I heard the name we had chosen for our baby being spoken to another woman's child; when my periods resumed and I packed my maternity clothes away; when I saw new babies, or friends announced new pregnancies; when my baby's due-date came and went unnoticed by most; and when my friends and family showed a thousand little kindnesses... then my broken heart throbbed with fresh waves of pain – and I wept.

But every time I wept, I felt God's loving presence surround me with comfort. When I grieved, I felt him draw near and give me strength to carry on for the day, and then the next day, and then the next. It felt like he was carrying me through the valley for a while, and then it felt like he walked next to me, still carrying my grief as I leaned on him. And eventually I felt my heart was healed enough to start to emerge out of the valley. I knew I would never forget my baby, and there is still a tender place in my heart today for the baby I never met, whom I look forward to embracing in Heaven one day. But I have no doubt God healed my heart over time by walking with me through the valley of the shadow of death, every step of the way.

I grew closer to him in that time than ever before and discovered how truly close he is to those who mourn. Never in a million years would I have chosen to lose my baby. And yet in the middle of all the pain and loss I found the greatest treasure of a deepened friendship with God, and for that I will always be thankful.

Losing my baby was the most painful thing I ever experienced…
BUT GOD drew closer than ever to comfort me.

CHAPTER 13

Miracle Rescue

It took over a year after the miscarriage to be able to conceive again. I still delighted in my little boy, but I knew God had promised multiple children, so not only was every period a traumatic visual reminder of my recent loss, but each time it was a fresh challenge to my faith that God would bless us again.

We continued to lead in the church, and a day came when the leadership team all went down to London for a training conference. I was still emotionally a little raw, but stronger by now, and it was an excellent conference. As the speaker concluded his message, he released a prophetic word to those there. "God wants to restore his promises to those who have been waiting a long time," he said, and as he uttered those words, God spoke to my heart: *"That includes your babies, Rachel. I have not forgotten."*

That night Mike and I stayed in a hotel in London while my parents babysat for us at home. And that night our new little promise was conceived. A few weeks later we discovered that I was pregnant again, and we were thrilled – but this time there was an element of fear that I had to keep managing until we got to the 12-week scan. Thankfully this time there was no empty space on the screen, and just as our first 12-week scan had been utterly beautiful, this time round the scan was an utter relief – quickly followed by huge joy.

The pregnancy followed a very similar pattern to my first: bananas, marmite, a more rapidly expanding belly, and even more exhaustion, now I had a non-napping three-year-old to manage. With the 12-week scan out of the way, I relaxed and enjoyed the pregnancy almost as much as the first one. We discovered at 20 weeks that we were having another boy and were overjoyed once more – a brother for Joshua seemed like perfection!

One morning near the end of the pregnancy I woke after a nightmare involving lots of dead animals. I couldn't shake the feeling of horror and dread, and as the day went on it seemed to me that my baby was not moving as much as usual. I phoned my sister – a midwife at the local hospital – thinking I was probably being silly and imagining things, but she calmly told me to go straight to the ward so they could monitor the baby, just to be on the safe side. All the way there I kept praying, and as I prayed I felt a strong need to pray for the umbilical cord to stay loose and away from my baby's neck. Once I got to the ward the staff were lovely and reassured me that I had done exactly the right thing – that they would far rather be bothered by a false alarm than miss a genuine problem. Happily, mine turned out to be the former. The adrenaline now running through my body seemed to have woken the baby up, and all the monitors showed he was happy and well.

That Christmas was a happy one. We kept Christmas Eve quietly, just going for a walk with family and remembering our little Heaven-baby who had died two years previously. On Christmas Day my belly was so huge I rested my plate on it to eat Christmas dinner as I couldn't reach the table. Not so much blooming as fit to burst!

Our second live son was born in January 2006. He was a bit late (a few days after his due date), but completely fine. My waters broke around teatime and over the next two hours my contractions got closer and closer together, until we felt we needed to go to hospital. Just after we put Josh to bed, Mike phoned my parents, and they came to babysit. I was examined when we got to the maternity ward and told I wasn't in active labour: despite all the contractions, my cervix wasn't dilated enough yet. I was so disappointed – it sure felt like labour to me! The midwife kindly gave me the option of going home and waiting there or staying for a cup of tea first, and then she would check again to see if there was any progress. Thankfully I chose to stay, because she had not been out of the room for long when the contractions intensified, and I had a sudden feeling of 'I'm not doing this anymore'. As soon as I recognised that thought crossing my mind, I knew I was transitioning into active labour. Within minutes I was ready to push, and I turned to Mike in a panic. "Get the midwife back now!"

She came rushing in, took in the situation with a single

glance, and pulled her gloves on – but she never got a chance to examine me again, because my baby was clearly coming. He was born less than an hour after I had arrived.

I had wanted a 'domino' birth – where the community midwife comes into hospital with you to deliver the baby and then takes you straight home after. However, although the ward had called my lovely community midwife when I got to hospital, she only got there just in time to see the baby delivered. She had been driving to the hospital when the police pulled her over on a random stop, and because her car was brand new, she couldn't figure out how to wind down the window to talk to them. They found this suspicious, so it took her a while to convince them it was all above board and for them to send her on her way. Meanwhile, my baby wasn't waiting for anyone, and his head was emerging just as our midwife walked in. Thankfully the hospital midwife had it all in hand.

After the birth was over and we were recovering, the late comer shared her story and we all laughed. Then she turned her attention back to our beautiful new-born and mused, "That was the longest umbilical cord I have ever seen!"

A chill suddenly ran through me as I remembered my dream of weeks before, the reduced movements of my unborn baby, and the feeling of needing to pray for the cord. I don't know if it had been an issue or would have been an issue, but the fact that it was so long and did not wrap around his neck seemed remarkable to me, and I thanked God even more for the safe delivery of my new miracle son.

Our community midwife sorted out the paperwork so we could get back home quickly in the early hours before Joshua even woke up. The whole thing had happened while he was still asleep, so when he woke in the morning and came into our bedroom, he found us with his new baby brother, and was thrilled!

We were overjoyed with our growing family and soon managed to find a new routine, helped by Josh starting preschool at the independent school that our church had started.

Early one autumn afternoon, I was attempting to tidy up downstairs when I heard the unmistakable sounds of baby Ben (now about 10 months old) waking up from his nap. I gladly left the cleaning and went upstairs to retrieve him from his cot, picking him up and indulging in the soft downiness of his hair against my cheek as he nestled into me. We started to make our way downstairs, but I had forgotten that at the top of the stairs was a little collection of toys waiting to be taken down. I had put them there earlier that morning while tidying, ignoring an inner nudge suggesting it might not be a good place to leave them, and had then been distracted and forgotten them. As I carried my precious baby to the staircase, I accidentally stepped on a toy car in the pile, and I completely lost my footing. The car – and my feet – shot backwards and my head was thrown forwards, resulting in me, and Ben in my arms, being propelled head-first down the flight of stairs. I can't say that I had time for my whole life to flash before me, but as my head went past my feet, hurtling towards the seven-foot floor-to-ceiling glass window at the bottom of the stairs, I had two split-second thoughts...

First: there was no way either of us could survive this. We were going to die or be very badly injured.

And second: there was only one person who could save us.

So I lifted my voice to cry out to the only one who could help: "Je…"

But before I could even utter the second syllable of Jesus' name, the impossible happened. One nanosecond we were mid-air and upside-down, plummeting towards an inevitable crash-landing through a huge pane of glass – and the next, we were sitting at the bottom of the stairs completely unharmed: window intact, not a bruise or a scratch anywhere, and my little blue-eyed Ben still safe in my arms, blinking up at me as if to ask what was going on. The only hint that anything had happened at all was my heart thumping fiercely with all the adrenaline now rushing through it as I sat there, struggling to comprehend what had just taken place: God, how did you do that?

Did he stop time to carry us from a place of extreme peril to one of safety? Did he transfer us instantly from one position to another? Did he command an angel or two to catch us and move us to safety in a flash? I have no idea (though I do hope I get to see an action replay once I get to Heaven). All I know is, it was impossible. I was in an impossible situation – I called on Jesus (who was so ready to rescue us he didn't even wait for me to finish his name) – and we were saved.

As the adrenaline faded and my heartbeat returned to normal, I remembered something that overwhelmed me with fresh thanks: the whole thing was my own fault. I was the one who had put the toys in a dangerous place; I was the one who ignored the inner voice of warning that it wasn't a good place to put them; I was the one who didn't look where I was going. But none of that stopped God from saving us.

I had foolishly put myself and my baby into a place of great danger…
BUT GOD miraculously rescued us.

CHAPTER 14

Heartbreak Healed

With the curse of infertility apparently no longer in effect, Mike and I were on a roll. Just a few months after Ben's first birthday we discovered I was pregnant again… and this new baby's due date was Christmas Eve! I was doubly delighted, not just for the blessing of another pregnancy, but as a close friend said at the time, it seemed to be a divine gift to redeem that date from the pain of losing our previous baby. Our friends and family were delighted again for us.

I now had two small sons at home, and much as I wanted to slow down and savour the knowledge of the new baby growing inside me, I was just too busy. I prayed when I could, but often had to content myself with just knowing God was still my friend and delighting with me at the joyful chaos of life in our family home.

With two successful pregnancies under our belts, and a recent miraculous experience demonstrating God's protection, I was probably a bit complacent. The first months passed uneventfully, and we went to the 12-week scan excited to see our newest unborn child. But the sonographer's professionally blank face gave it away before we even saw the screen: there was a problem. They checked and double-checked the dates with me in case the pregnancy was not as far along as I had thought, but I knew my dates were right.

They showed us the screen. Again it revealed that hideous blank space where my baby should have been. And again the choice was offered: have my womb scraped out, or go home with an invitation to a follow-up scan in a couple of weeks, just in case the dates did turn out to be wrong. But we knew that was just their way of trying to be gentle over what seemed to be inevitable. I was not taken in; I knew my baby had died. The womb scrape still wasn't an option in my mind, and we chose to go home – but this time I was not planning to comply with nature. After our first miscarriage I had come to feel a kind of righteous indignation that it was the enemy – who the Bible calls Satan – who had killed my baby then, and I regretted not fighting back with faith against him then. In fact I had made a vow to God that never again would I take an attack from the enemy lying down. And now, even amid my devastation at the news we had received, a fierce resolve arose within me: I was going to fight back with faith.

I knew I'd been caught off-guard and had a lot of ground to cover. I also knew that what I was aiming my faith at was impossible – and naturally speaking I did not have a lot of time to play with. Our previous miscarriage had taught me that haemorrhaging would be likely to commence soon if I did not get my miracle. Nevertheless, I set my faith high. Mike agreed, and we made the decision not to tell anyone except Mark and Sandra who we knew would agree with our faith and pray in agreement with us. And bless them, they did. I think they were surprised, but immediately agreed, nonetheless. All we told anyone else who asked was that the scan did not go as expected, and we had another one scheduled for a couple of weeks' time.

Then I shut myself away to pray. Obviously, I still had Josh and Ben to care for, and I gladly did so. But every other spare waking minute was spent researching accounts of people being raised from the dead, reading the promises of God from the Bible out loud, praying in tongues, and speaking blessings of life and resurrection over my baby. I fought with everything I had and refused to quit.

But a day came when I started to lose blood. Just a little at first, and I fought even harder to pray and believe. However soon I was haemorrhaging badly, and I ended up in Accident and Emergency going into hypovolemic shock because of the ferocity of the blood-loss. Again, the doctors worked feverishly to stem the flow, hooking me up to a fluid drip because my blood pressure had dropped to dangerously low levels. It looked like I would need a transfusion, but I did not want one because at the time there were several cases of MRSA in the hospital, and I felt too vulnerable, so I prayed for the bleeding to stop. Mike called the church to pray, and they prayed the same. Finally, just in time, the doctors brought the haemorrhaging under control – and I was taken to the ward, with no transfusion needed. But there, reality hit: I had lost the battle for my baby.

Physically I was very weak from the blood loss. Emotionally I was very weak from the grief of losing my baby. And spiritually I was utterly spent. I had fought with all I had for my miracle, but it had not happened. I had failed and felt utterly defeated and alone.

I was released home after a day or so, under strict instructions not to lift a finger. Thankfully we were blessed with wonderful friends and family who sorted us out with meals, cleaning, and so on. While the children were awake, I was able to concentrate on enjoying their cuddles and being thankful for them all over again. It was only in the dark hours of night that my confusion and grief would again overwhelm me. Having fought so hard in faith this time it seemed an even greater defeat than before, and I was really struggling. I didn't know how to even talk to God about it – I was too confused, and I was devastated at both the loss of my baby and by not knowing why my battle had been lost.

After a week or so when I was strong enough to resume some of my normal routine, I started doing the school run again. That first morning back when I dropped Josh off to his class, I dropped into the office to say hello to Mark and Sandra, doing my best to get 'back to normal'. During the conversation Mark made a comment about the baby I just lost that I'm sure he believed would be comforting, but to my grieving heart it was the most insensitive thing he could have said. I hastily said my goodbyes and left, dashing to the nearest room (the school kitchen) where I promptly burst into heaving sobs on the shoulder of a lovely friend. So much for 'back to normal' – who was I kidding? My friend, who had walked her own path with grief, was kind and understanding, and hugged me tight. Somehow though I knew that to really overcome this I had to go back to Mark and Sandra, because I felt they had the faith and authority as leaders to pray with me. Even though Mark's words had hurt me, I knew he was not the true cause of my pain. So, my lovely friend arranged for toddler Ben to visit the pre-schoolers class (taught by another friend of mine) while I headed back to the office. They were surprised to see me again, but kindly stopped everything as they saw my distress.

"I can't do this anymore," I sobbed. "I just can't carry on like this."

And they prayed with me immediately.

There and then I experienced a deep sense of God's compassionate presence with me. With my faithful friends by my side, I released the pain of all the hours and days I had spent fighting for my baby. I gave God the fear and failure I had felt in the hospital as I barely held on to consciousness, I gave him the unconsciously insensitive comment that had just brutally exposed my pain afresh, and I gave him my utterly broken heart. And somehow, amid all that chaos, pain and brokenness, he gave me back my heart – completely healed. I felt peace for the first time since the scan – but peace on a deeper level than I had ever known before. It was a victorious peace. I had lost the battle for my baby – but Jesus had won the war for my heart, and my relationship with God was restored.

By the time I got home with Ben, a 10-minute drive later, I felt utterly new. I had joy and strength. I had gone from dragging myself around trying to function normally, to dancing around my front room praising God. When I went to church that weekend Mark was astonished at the change. He wasn't the only one. I knew God had worked a miracle in my heart.

This wasn't denial – it was something else. I was still sad about the loss of my baby, still missed her (I believe God showed us she was a girl), and six months later we still had to make another choice to celebrate Christmas without letting it be tainted by a now doubly tragic association. But my broken heart was simply and impossibly not broken any more.

With the first miscarriage God had healed my broken heart gradually over many months – one step at a time, walking through it with me in a way that proved him to be the most faithful, present friend I would ever know. But this time he healed me of my broken heart in an instant. It was amazing. Some might say it was better than the first time, because who wouldn't want instant healing, given the choice? But although I was and still am grateful for both kinds of healing, the first one was when I really got to know Jesus more deeply as my friend, and that is a treasure I would not give up for anything. Either way though, I am grateful. Sometimes God delivers people *through* a situation, and sometimes he delivers people *out of* a situation. I count myself blessed to have experienced both.

I was completely devastated...
BUT GOD healed my broken heart in an instant.

CHAPTER 15

Coming Out Fighting

After my second miscarriage, Christmas Eve was now doubly poignant because of it being my fourth baby's due date, as well as the anniversary of my first miscarriage. I had even more reason to cling to my decision not to let the memories rob me of the opportunity to celebrate with my loved ones, but it wasn't as easy as simply choosing to be happy. I tried, but invariably found that 'toughing it out' would result in emotional overload and inevitable break-down at some point over the holiday. However, I came to realise that it really helped me to cope with the full-on craziness of the season if I kept one day quiet for remembering my Heaven-babies. And it made sense to me for that day to be Christmas Eve. So we started a tradition of going for a gentle family outdoor walk somewhere peaceful in the afternoon, driving home past as many lit-up houses as the children could spot, having pizza delivered for tea (no cooking for Mum to do – hooray!) then opening a Christmas Eve box for the boys, filled with new Christmassy pyjamas, new mugs, hot chocolate, squirty cream, marshmallows and peppermint sticks, plus a bag of popcorn and a DVD of a new cartoon retelling of the Nativity story. Over the years Christmas Eve has become the whole family's favourite part of Christmas – what started with tragedy has become a cherished tradition – but in 2007 it was just my way of coping and giving myself space that allowed me to then engage fully with the festivities of the days that followed.

A day or two before the start of 2008 we met with the whole leadership team of the church to pray for each other. One of my friends there prophesied that there were some unfulfilled promises in some of our lives that God wanted to bring to pass, and I instantly felt a warmth in my spirit, like God was saying he hadn't forgotten his promise for multiple children. In my mind two living babies didn't count as 'multiple', and inside me there was a constant, unsatisfied desire for more, so we kept trying, kept hoping and kept praying… until a few weeks later in January 2008, we were overjoyed to discover our newest baby was on the way!

I didn't allow myself to get complacent this time though. Experience had taught me that I had to fight for my babies, and this time I was not going to take any chance of letting the enemy kill any more. So from the first day I saw those two beautiful lines on the stick, I went to war. It was the only pregnancy that we didn't announce to all our friends and family from day one. That wasn't because I was afraid – far from it: I was ready for the fight! But I felt that others might not be. If we had told those who loved us, they might have worried on our behalf, might have spoken out their concerns or put their fears into words. And it could seem excessive to some, but I didn't want anyone speaking anything negative over my new baby. I didn't want to be distracted from my fight of faith by having to pretend not to notice sympathetic or worried faces, or deal with other people's fears. The only people we told were Mark and Sandra, knowing they would pray along with our faith and not give way to fear.

It was very difficult keeping the news from all our family, so I just focused on getting up early every morning to pray, speaking in tongues (because I thought the Holy Spirit would know how to pray better than I did), and speaking blessings of life and health over my unborn baby. Josh and Ben kept me very busy all the rest of the time while they were awake, and then when they went to bed, I would read the Bible and keep declaring trust in God's blessing over my baby. From time to time a fearful thought would cross my mind, and straight away I would reject it: I'd refuse to dwell on it or even entertain it, but instead would determinedly start praising and thanking God again for the life in my womb. This routine continued without fail until a few days before the 12-week scan.

I had woken early to pray as usual and was praying in tongues again, when I felt God speak to my heart: "*You've done it – you've won the battle and your baby is safe.*" I was so locked on to the fight that I continued with my battle routine for the next few days. But the day of the scan came, and I went in faith, refusing to give in to fear. Mike stood near the sonographer so that even though I couldn't see the screen until she had taken her measurements, he could – and I could see his grin right away. Eventually she turned it to face me, and there was my beautiful unborn baby kicking away, as healthy and lively as could be.

We couldn't wait any longer to tell everyone, and quickly made up for the weeks of total silence with several months of celebration. I sometimes light-heartedly say that I overdid the praying because when our new baby was born he was far and away my biggest baby (at 10lbs 11oz), and it quickly became apparent that he was the most vibrant, energetic and full-of-life child that I have ever met. There was just one difference to the previous two births. After Joshua was delivered, even though they had to use forceps to help him out because he had been facing the wrong way, I lay on the bed cuddling him and said, "Yeah, I would do that again." Nobody asked me, I just spontaneously said it. Then again after Ben's speedy birth, I cuddled him close and said, "Yep, I'm not finished yet!"

This time though after Daniel, my newest and biggest baby, made his way into the world, I merely said, "We'll see, shall we?" And that feeling of wanting, needing, *having* to have more babies simply never came back. I was satisfied – our family was complete.

The big family that God had promised was threatened many times…
BUT GOD taught me how to fight and win.

CHAPTER 16

Co-Parenting with God

The years between 2001 and 2010 were mostly spent either pregnant or breastfeeding, or at least changing nappies... and I loved it! Almost a decade of seeing the answers to my prayers come into being. I loved it all, but still, it was a real challenge dealing with all the usual mum issues, from the big stuff of 'How do I juggle all the different needs of my children and still get time with my husband?' to simply 'How am I going to fit in having a shower?' And I especially missed having the luxury of getting time to hang out with God without distraction. But even without a regular prayer or Bible study time, he was still my friend – and in those nine years and beyond, God showed me how to 'abide' in him. Maybe I didn't have time to give him my sole attention as I would have liked, but I learned to focus on and enjoy his presence even while changing a nappy or pureeing endless little pots of food, and especially while rocking a precious little one back to sleep in the middle of the night.

Mike and I were tired. A lot. But so happy! Those years were such precious times – the fulfilment of God's promised children, and I never forgot it. Even when dealing with a screaming baby, I was thankful – though sometimes I had to remind myself of that fact! And motherhood unlocked a new fierceness in me that I never dreamed could be there. I had always been somewhat of a pacifist – albeit one with deeply held, passionate beliefs – but now I knew with absolute certainty that I had it in me to kill if anyone threatened my babies. The maternal instinct is a powerful force, and it taught me a lot about how overwhelming God's love is for us. As I realised I would give my life for my kids without hesitation it hit me all over again how Jesus did just that for us. There's nothing like having children of your own to make you appreciate God's deep love for his kids.

I prayed for my boys often, speaking blessings over them, and praying that God would lead them to know him just as I did. Once I held my first baby in my arms, a long-held fear of mine re-emerged, that it was not possible to be the kind of perfect parent that my children deserved (that every child deserves). Having done the Family Life Skills course back in Ely, I was very aware of the emotional damage that can be done unconsciously by even the smallest flaw in a parent, and it really bothered me to think that I would inevitably cause some emotional damage to my perfect new babies, however hard I tried not to. So I prayed, and told God I hated not being a perfect mother and that I was scared of the impact it would have on our children. He gently told me I would never be perfect this side of eternity – and that yes, it was sadly inevitable that I would make mistakes with my beautiful boys. But, he said, if I did my best to love them and if I introduced them to him, he would heal them as they grew up and took their wounds to him, just as he had healed me. It was such a relief to be reminded that before they were my children, they were his; that he desired friendship with them every bit as much as he did with me; that his plans for them were good plans, and he was – is – well able to bring those plans to pass.

So Mike and I prayed for them to come to know him as their friend, and we taught them about him and prayed with them. It wasn't something we did as routine every day, but it was a natural part of our lives. Sometimes I worried that in the busyness of life we were neglecting the benefits of a daily routine and not doing enough to introduce them to him, but then in 2009 something happened that reassured me God was speaking to them too.

Josh was now seven years old, in school and generally a cheerful little boy. But one evening after I had put him to bed, he came downstairs again, having had a bad dream. It took a while to persuade him to tell me about it, but eventually it came out that a friend at school had been telling him all about the new swine flu that was going around – this friend was rather fascinated by it and had shared all sorts of frightening predictions of death and suffering that the media had been speculating on. At the time Josh ran off to play with someone else to distract himself, but it obviously stuck with him, and by the dark hours of bedtime, alone with his thoughts, he was gripped with fear.

I prayed with him and did my best to soothe his fears with platitudes, speaking of the tiny chances of it hurting us, and sent him back to bed. However, he could not sleep, and got up again several times, really distressed, and scared of what he would dream. Each time either Mike or I said a prayer, had a cuddle and put him back to sleep – but by the fourth or fifth time we were running out of ideas, and I silently cried out for help: obviously what I was doing was not meeting my seven-year-old's needs. He needed help and I was failing to give it. In that moment of silently reaching to God for help as I soothed my boy back to bed, something suddenly switched in me: the Holy Spirit spoke to me and reminded me that fear was from the enemy, and that Jesus had delegated authority to us to deal with it. I realised the enemy was tormenting Josh and I did not have to take it. Now I meant business: until that point my prayers had been shallow platitudes spoken from habit but not really connecting with God, but this time I took authority over the fear that was trying to take over my boy and commanded it to go. I spoke blessings of peace to his heart, and sound sleep in Jesus' Name. My own prayers had initially been a feeble religious ritual, but now the Holy Spirit was moving through me. I knew this prayer was different and powerful, and I went downstairs feeling it was settled.

Sure enough, Josh slept through the night without a single murmur. In the morning he seemed calm and cheerful. "Did you have any more bad dreams?" I asked a little reluctantly, not wanting to remind him of his previous night's fears, but I needn't have been concerned.

He smiled peacefully and said to me, "I had a dream and

there was this angel with an enormous shield hovering over our roof. So now I'm not scared."

What a beautiful picture God had given my son! And what a beautiful reminder to me, that not only was God willing to help me when my parenting was not enough, but that he had his own relationship with my children and was well able to speak to them directly.

I failed often at being the perfect mother I wanted to be...
BUT GOD parented even when I couldn't.

CHAPTER 17

The End of an Era

That first decade of the third millennium was such a blessing to live through! Our children were in a good school, our church was thriving, and life was good. We had strong friendships and the true blessing of family around us. We felt we were on a good, solid path in our life and ministry. But as we approached the end of the decade, little did we suspect that the ground beneath our feet was about to be significantly shaken.

One day, when Mark returned from a trip to America, we contacted him to leave a 'welcome home' message after his flight landed. He didn't reply for a few days, and we were confused because it was not like him. Over those few days the concern over why Mark was not communicating with us seemed to bring questions to a head that Mike and I had been doing our best to suppress.

For a while we had been fighting a restless kind of uncertainty. We knew God had called us as armour-bearers and assistant pastors, and were still wholly committed to both, but we had also been starting to wonder if Mark and Sandra still felt the same. We couldn't identify anything in particular causing us to feel this way, but still it niggled, and was unsettling us both, leading us to ask if God had changed his mind. We prayed about it more than once, but each time we felt our call was still there, and that we were dealing with spiritual interference from the enemy, though we couldn't identify it any more clearly than that. So we prayed some more, but the questions did not go away and those few days after Mark's return seemed to provoke even greater uncertainty and confusion.

Eventually, within the week, Mark called an evening leadership team meeting. That morning Mike and I prayed again, but where before God had reassured us that his calling was unchanged, this time he spoke clearly to our hearts, simply asking us to let go of it all: everything he had called us to with Mark and Sandra; all the areas where we were bearing fruit and being fulfilled; and to give it all back to him. It felt shockingly sudden and didn't make sense, but God's leading was clear, so we prayed together, and told him we willingly gave it all back to him. And God took our confused obedience and exchanged it for a real peace that settled in our hearts. We still didn't understand, but we no longer needed to – we knew we could trust him whatever came, and that was what carried us through.

Mike and I went to the team meeting that evening, still

feeling peace but also looking forward to hopefully getting some answers that would lay to rest the uneasy feelings we had been having. However, not long after the meeting started, seemingly out of nowhere, Mark asked us to step down as assistant pastors. The rest of the team were clearly shocked, but all I could think was how thankful I was that God had so mercifully prepared us for what was to come. The confusion was greater than ever, but somehow God had given us a peace that was greater still! It felt like what the Bible calls a 'peace that goes beyond understanding'[12], that we were so grateful for, then and through the season that followed.

It was a deeply painful time. The rejection that I was so familiar with from my youth tried to rear its ugly head again. Where previously I had felt listened to, and our contribution valued, now I felt my voice had been silenced, and my offering of service rejected. It would be a long time before it was restored. Our friendship with Mark and Sandra was tested as Mike and I were tempted to give in to indignation and self-pity. I couldn't understand how the calling we had received from God could be so abruptly ended. Over and over I asked God if he had changed his mind. Had we done something wrong? Was this his will, and if so, why did it feel so confusing? How should we pray against the attack that we felt had been unleashed against us all?

But all God would say during those times was to keep trusting in him and walking with him – that he would lead us through the storm. So that is what we tried to do. We didn't understand what was going on, but we knew God's principles of forgiveness and love would stand against every temptation.

---

[12] Philippians 4:7

And his beautiful peace stayed with us even through all the very real pain and confusion, and kept our hearts from total devastation. We didn't want to get offended, knowing that to be one of the enemy's favourite ways to tempt God's people. So we stayed in the church and even though our opportunities were now limited, we tried to bless the people there still.

This was for two main reasons: firstly, God had not led us anywhere else; and secondly, there were many in the church who were growing increasingly hurt and confused. We loved Mark and Sandra and wanted them to succeed. And we loved the people and wanted to help them. Many people, including some of the previous leadership team, were now leaving and finding new churches, but Mike and I had been there since the very beginning. We had given our lives to serve the church practically as well as spiritually, and they knew us well. Many were confused and looking to us to figure out how to respond to all the changes happening. And there was no way that we wanted to lead them into being offended. If God was going to call us or any of the congregation to a different church, we wanted it to be with clean hearts.

Over the course of the next couple of years, the church dwindled. We were still confused, but clung to God's peace. Eventually we came to a season when the church was only meeting altogether once a month. On one of those days we gathered, now in much smaller numbers than before; we sang together, we listened to a sermon, but it seemed to me that all the previously dynamic life of the Holy Spirit had gone. And as I sat at the back trying to keep my youngest child quiet and praying for all the people who were faithfully struggling on, I suddenly heard the voice of God speak right into my heart, saying, "*You're not helping anyone by staying, you know.*" And in that instant, I knew. It was now time to trust him with the people we loved there – Mark and Sandra, the other remaining leaders, and those left in the congregation – and that he was now releasing us from the church we still loved, to start seeking him for a future elsewhere.

We felt hurt and disoriented as everything we thought we knew was stripped away…
BUT GOD's peace carried us through it all.

CHAPTER 18

Unexpected Blessings

Around the same time as our church family was coming to an end, there were other changes going on in our own family.

By 2011, all our boys were in our church-run independent school (Daniel was in the preschool) and I was teaching a small class on the same site – it seemed ideal. We wanted our children to have the socialisation opportunities of school, and seeing as our church ran a school where I also worked, it was a no-brainer for us. I could still be near my kids (albeit not teaching them myself), and they could have a school experience, just smaller and more nurturing than state school, which I had no peace about. Josh settled in quite easily – his best friend was in his class which helped, though he found some subjects boring. When Ben started there he really enjoyed preschool: he had two teachers whom he adored and who loved him back. But during his first year of 'proper' school, he changed. His class wasn't that large, but it might have been easier if it had been – at least he would have had a larger group of friends to choose from. He really struggled with being the youngest in the class, which covered a few years in age range, and he just switched off when presented with work that wasn't engaging. Consequently, he was regularly told off for not doing his work or for drawing on the table, and it wasn't long before he had developed a kind of self-fulfilling reputation as the 'naughty kid' even though he wasn't naughty, just unhappy. It was the most painful thing for a parent to watch: over the space of a term he went from being a happy, chatty, just-so-sweet little boy, to a genuinely depressed five-year-old. He completely turned in on himself and barely spoke or laughed anymore.

Of course, Mike and I prayed. We had already been dreaming dreams of buying a home where we could keep chickens and home educate our family, but it just seemed like a far-off fantasy. Meanwhile our precious middle boy was now severely unhappy. We cried out for wisdom, prayed for breakthrough, and searched for answers.

At the end of term, we all heaved a sigh of relief and settled down to enjoy the Christmas holidays. It seemed to cheer him up a little, but that wasn't to last. Things really came to a head a couple of weeks into the new term, over his sixth birthday.

There was a girl in his class who had a birthday the same weekend but was a year older. I asked her mum which day she was having her party as I knew Ben would want to ask the same friends from their small class, so we chose the following day for his party. But in the week before his birthday, I discovered that the little girl concerned had spoken to all the children and told them not to go to his party at all, just hers, even though I had made sure they didn't clash. I have no idea how she managed to persuade them – I thought it was just childish nonsense – but sure enough, when the day came, only one of his school friends turned up (and I will love her forever for it). Somehow, we managed to make the party lots of fun, but I was more devastated than Ben himself – I wept in private over that rejection of him. There was no point blaming the little girl – it seemed spiteful, but she was only seven, and I had no idea of her background. But it completely broke the illusion of school socialisation being good for the boys. The so-called 'socialisation' had actually worked against my sweet boy: being in school was destroying him before our eyes.

Mike and I talked and prayed some more – this time newly open to an option that we had previously discounted, and praying again for our dream home, chickens and all. And as we prayed, God answered, saying firmly, "*You don't need chickens to home educate!*" His tone was clear: he was leading us into home education. I asked him if it was just for our Ben's sake, but he told us no, this was a blessing that he wanted to give the whole family. Josh was doing OK at school, but was mostly bored, and his daily homework had become a battleground that was devastating all our family time – both evenings and weekends – as we spent all our spare time trying to cajole him into getting it done. Daniel was happy in preschool, but we were already seeing signs that he would also struggle with the more structured nature of 'big school'.

I had some major concerns over home education. Socialisation wasn't one of them anymore, but at times it did feel like a risky experiment with my kids' futures at stake. However, God's leading was strong and clear, and he promised to guide us through it all. And as we finally yielded to what we realised God had been trying to lead us to all along, the sense of peace and relief that came over us was immense. I worked at the boys' school so I was committed to working to the end of term, which meant the boys had to stay there too. It was horrible watching Ben continue to struggle, but we all managed to keep going until March 2012 when we left for good.

That Easter holiday was such a happy time, without the stress of school hanging over us. And on the first day of term when we did not have to go back to school, I felt a huge, tangible sense of relief. Gone was the sergeant-major persona I had to adopt to get all the boys up, dressed, fed and washed, with full lunchboxes and homework bags in their hands, in time for the school run. Gone was all the stress and pressure of endless and uninspiring homework, spiteful classmates, and sad children. We stayed in our pyjamas that first day and had the most delightful day at home, enjoying each other's company and learning for fun! And truthfully, our home education journey for at least the next four years (until our eldest started studying towards exams) followed pretty much the same joyful path. We had fun with kitchen science, made up stories, baked all sorts of treats, created arty projects, held poetry picnics, carried out STEM experiments, and undertook projects around whatever subjects the boys were interested in. We assembled jigsaws, played numerous educational board games, read endless books, and watched too many documentaries to remember. We even found online programmes that made maths fun! We enjoyed frequent nature walks and outings to historic places and found many local home education groups where the boys could socialise in a safe environment: hanging out with and learning alongside friends, but with parents usually nearby if children needed to come and ask for help navigating a tricky social problem. We had no idea how rich and fulfilling it would be to home educate our boys, but those years were jam-packed with blessing!

Josh and Daniel loved it immediately and threw themselves into whatever we did with great gusto. It took a while for Ben to really recover: the first group we went to, he stayed behind my legs, too subdued to join in. But gradually we started to see him relax, and within a couple of months I felt we had our beautiful boy back. His sensitivity to others' feelings was allowed to bloom in a safe place and he became one of the most well-liked children in any group that we went to. And without the stress and pressure of structured school lessons he was allowed to investigate the things he enjoyed at his own pace. Maths was no longer a chore, but fun; his language skills flourished as he became a devoted bookworm, and his creative, fun-loving personality really came to the fore. Each of the boys' personalities developed beautifully before our eyes, and we came to appreciate that through home education we had been given the best gift of time to really enjoy each other.

We were ignorant over what we were missing out on…
BUT GOD had unexpected blessings prepared for us!

Chapter 19

Into the Unknown

Without a home church to belong to, the years that followed could have been difficult, but God used them to heal some areas where we needed refreshing. The boys and I were thriving in home education, but Mike was still working, so having our weekends 'church-free' gave us a lovely opportunity to enjoy being family, without endless meetings to organise and prepare for. We felt God was leading us to rest and recover, and we ended up spending over a year without a church family. It was hard, but we were grateful for the space to heal.

Eventually though, a situation occurred in the home education community where a person whom I had befriended turned against me and became quite nasty. Even though most of that community were truly lovely and very supportive of each other, it made me realise I was missing a place of spiritual sanctuary – a church family. Mike and I prayed about it and felt led to visit our local Vineyard[13] church. We really liked the church and felt God's presence there, so we took the leaders out for a meal and asked if they were OK with us coming along just to receive ministry. We had never done that before – we had always believed in being fully committed to actively serving church family however we could – but God had spoken clearly to us about not rushing back into any kind of leadership, and just to enjoy and be restored by being in fellowship again. There were some fun groups for the children to attend, and a mid-week homegroup with some truly lovely people that Mike and I joined. We were there for about a year or so, and I will always be grateful for the generosity of the leaders in allowing us to just receive the blessing and rest that God had for us.

In 2013 and 2014 both of my grandparents died, after which Mike and I started to feel a distinct restlessness that we could not ignore, and it quickly became apparent that God was indeed calling us away.

Initially it was no more than a strong call to leave – we had no idea where to go, only that God was calling us as He had called Abraham in the book of Genesis, to leave this place and go to a land that He was going to show us. So even though we had no idea where we were going, Mike and I agreed that we both felt a clear call to leave and started preparing. We had been in that house for over five years – the longest our family had lived in any house – and loved it there. The garden backed onto a strip of woodland where we had spent many happy hours watching foxes, badgers, muntjac and fallow deer. Our garden itself was home to many birds, grey and black squirrels, and a succession of poorly wild hedgehogs whom I had learned to rehabilitate and release back into the wild. We had no idea about all of that when we moved in, but God did. He knows how much I love wildlife and he knew what a blessing it would be to me there: it was my little haven. We had good relationships with the neighbours there too. I'd organised a couple of street parties and was extra blessed by a good friend moving into the house over the road – we were in and out of each other's houses all the time. The family next door became good friends too, with our children playing together often. And of course, my parents and my sister and her family still lived in Stevenage as well as many friends from our old and new churches. In short, there were plenty of blessings there and it was a huge wrench to leave – but we knew God was calling and we knew that if we stayed in a place where we were no longer meant to be, it would rapidly cease to be a blessing. We wanted what God wanted, and he obviously had another plan for us.

The logical first step seemed to be to figure out where to go, but God had said he would show us *as we went*, so we knew we had first to get ready, to be able to follow every instruction promptly. So even without a known destination, we simply started to declutter. Having lived there for five years with three young home educated boys and a bevy of hedgehogs to care for, we had acquired a LOT of stuff. Thankfully I do love the decluttering process. There was a lot to do, and my time was mostly taken up with my boys, but it was both satisfying and a very clear way of showing our commitment to the move. It was our way of saying, "Yes, Lord, we're ready to obey."

As we did so, our hearts started to focus on the West Midlands where Mike's parents still lived. My Bible readings repeatedly took me to verses that spoke about the importance of family, and people going back to the land of their fathers, so we felt that God had purpose for us in the place where Mike had originally come from.

Of course, that meant leaving my side of the family who had come to Stevenage to be with us, only for us to now leave them again. I really wasn't looking forward to telling them. I knew that my parents and grandparents' move to Stevenage had been very stressful, and my dad had consequently said that he would never move again but would be 'carried out of here in a box'. So even though we had left them behind previously when we left Stroud, somehow it seemed harder this time. But I felt God ask me to trust him, and I knew his plan must be good, so we went to speak to them.

They listened quietly but without pressure as we spoke, until I mentioned one of the areas we were considering, in the Malvern Hills. At this, my dad's ears pricked up and he started talking about his fond memories of the time he had spent working in that area long ago. Nowhere else at all appealing to them, but despite his much-repeated vow of never moving again, he suddenly did a total U-turn and announced that he could be very happy in Malvern! With him open to the idea, my mum also readily agreed to consider moving to Worcestershire with us, so with very little resistance we became two families looking for potential new homes. I went home with such a light heart that day – we had thought we were looking at leaving one side of the family to be with another, but it turned out so much better. I wasn't entirely relieved, as I knew I would really miss my sister, but when we went to see her and my brother-in-law I discovered God had an even better plan: as soon as we mentioned what was happening she said, "Well, you're not going without us!" – and we became three families looking for homes in the West Midlands!

My parents and sister were the first to get some free time to drive to Worcestershire. They drove to Malvern but somehow couldn't picture themselves moving there. However, when they drove further north in the county to where they had seen other potential houses, my mum and sister felt more of a confirmation from the Holy Spirit... and amazingly Dad agreed too! And as Mike and I looked at potential rental properties in Malvern, none of them seemed right, whereas we found a more northerly one in the same county that we loved. So, we started the tenancy application process.

By now we were packing boxes, sensing that when we found our house, we would need a rapid turnaround. We felt that God had given us a moving date (partly influenced by the end date of Mike's current work contract) so we had handed in our notice at our current house, and by the time we found the house we loved, we only had a few weeks left to go! However, the day after we started the application process I had a broken night's sleep, feeling somehow uneasy about the home we had chosen. When I woke the next morning, I asked God if he was behind my apprehension and trying to tell us something. I didn't hear a specific response, so I prayed again: "God, if this is not the house for us, will you please block the application?" That afternoon I had a phone call from the letting agent, apologising profusely but explaining that the landlady had decided to give her friend first refusal on it, and would we mind waiting. The sense of relief I felt told me everything I needed to know. We politely declined and started looking again, with extra urgency this time. Our moving-out date was quickly approaching, but we knew God must have somewhere for us, and it clearly wasn't the first one we had thought, so now we just needed to find it.

A day later a house appeared on the lettings list in Bewdley – a beautiful little market town in north Worcestershire. It seemed perfect. As a temporarily empty vicarage, it was huge, with a bedroom each for the boys and room for them to have their own den too, for their games console and vast quantity of home education resources. It was within walking distance of a play park and had a huge garden, and I loved it at first sight of the particulars. The only drawback was that it was a short-term lease (for six months) but we felt it was what we needed to get us into the county, there was nothing else suitable, and we were running out of time. So even though the letting agent said they would not be able to show him round, Mike and my dad drove the couple of hours there and then back again, just to have a look at the outside and peer through what windows they could. Mike sent a couple of photos, and video-called me, and we agreed: this was the one. We started the application that evening… and two weeks later we moved in! The whole move went so quickly in the end, I was really grateful for the advance warning we had been given to declutter and start packing even when we didn't know where we were going. We were so focused on getting there that it was only once we arrived at the end of October that we had a chance to draw breath… and realise that we were now in a place where we knew absolutely no-one and had to start building a new life.

That year we celebrated possibly my favourite Christmas ever: the house was big enough to fit all of us; my parents and sister's family all came to stay, and my brother and his family visited on Boxing Day. It was such a blessing to have everyone together under one roof! But once the fun of planning the Christmas celebrations had subsided and everyone had gone home, the new year felt very bleak. We had visited a local church a few times but although we liked it, didn't feel it was our 'home'. We were slowly making friends, but the home education community were more spread out and harder to connect with than the strong community we had left behind in Stevenage. Mike struggled to find a job, and I really struggled to find purpose in why we were there. I felt myself sliding down into a dark pit on the inside and couldn't seem to pull myself or pray myself out of it. For the first time in decades, I felt like my prayers weren't connecting with God – I couldn't find him in it all. And I felt lonely, so far away from my family. Mike's family were closer now, but not close enough to easily drop in, and I felt very alone, struggling even to find God, my best friend, in it all.

After a month or so, there came a weekend when my two best friends from Stevenage (one of whom was now living in Scotland) happened to visit at the same time. This was a rare treat, and I was extra pleased to see them. The three of us families went out for a walk together but although I tried to be jolly for their sake, my two friends realised something was very wrong. So later that evening they arranged for all our children to stay with the dads, and they took me out for a walk, just the three of us. They found a bench by the river, sat me down and prayed for me. Their presence alone was really comforting, and then at one point one of them prayed prophetically, affirming that my family and I were in the right place and God had a plan – that we weren't alone. As she prayed, I felt the darkness lift. I hadn't been able to name the bleak feeling I was experiencing, other than feeling generally depressed, but as she prayed, I realised I had been feeling hopeless. Without a vision for why we were there (other than generally obeying God), I'd had no hope or purpose – nothing to focus on. I have never been one of those people who can drift along without a raison d'être, and I had lost sight of the fact that it was so clearly God who had brought us here. Now, with the cloud lifted, I felt peaceful once more and able to trust God to guide our steps – and extra thankful for the friends he sent.

It wasn't long before my sister and her family moved into the area, and things felt better still. Very quickly after they moved in, a house nearby became available for sale that my parents loved and put an offer on – but before they could move in, Mike and I were given notice that our lease was up, and we needed to move – AGAIN! Even though we had known it would be a short-term lease I was very aware of how hard it was on the boys to go through the upheaval of having to move again so quickly. So I talked to God about it, and I felt him remind me that my boys were his kids too, and he knew how to bless them still. He told me to ask them to pray for a specific thing that they each wanted in our new house, and he would answer. Josh wanted to live somewhere near trees, Ben wanted another den as he loved the one in Bewdley, and Daniel wanted a dog! We had all wanted a dog for a while, but most rental places were averse to pets, so especially with the other boys' two requests it felt like a lot to ask. However, I reasoned that it was God's idea, so we prayed, making our requests, and waited for the answer.

Not long after we found details of a house that seemed expensive, but we felt prompted to go and view it. We pulled up onto the drive and spotted the trees bordering our garden and the field next to it – tick for Josh! As we made our way through the downstairs rooms we realised that one of the rooms would make a perfect den space for the boys – tick for Ben! The only question remaining was about getting a dog, and we decided to call the agents to ask when we got home. But as we made our way downstairs from seeing the beautiful views from the bedroom windows, we found the landlord at the bottom of the stairs. "Do you have any pets?" he asked.

Caught off guard, I slowly said, "Not yet—" preparing to ask if it would be OK.

But I didn't even get to ask him, as he promptly volunteered that we would be very welcome to get one! With all the boys' boxes ticked, I prayed, thanking God but expressing concern about the rental price. He simply said, *"This is where I am going to bless you,"* so we knew this was his plan, and he would provide. And that is exactly what he did!

It wasn't long before our family was joined by an eight-week-old puppy called Barney. The boys were immediately besotted. He was small enough to not scare them, crazy enough to be a fun playmate, and chilled enough to enjoy plenty of snuggles. We had the perfect field to exercise him in behind our garden, and a new chapter in our life started of full-time pet ownership. In the years since we have had Barney, I have lost count of the lessons God has taught me through him, not least about unconditional love and what it means to know someone who will always, ALWAYS be pleased to see you!

Shortly after we moved there, my parents finally moved into their new house too, and I started to feel much more settled. God had made it very clear that we were where he wanted us. Now we just needed to figure out what he wanted us to do there!

We had no idea where we were supposed to go (or why)...
BUT GOD took us on an adventure into bigger blessings.

CHAPTER 20

Reluctant Leader

Once we had spent a few months training our new puppy and getting him to the point where we could safely go out and leave him for a few hours, I found myself growing hungry for a new church family where we could 'get our hands dirty' and serve God's people.

We visited a few churches – some were very different in style to what we were used to, and we knew we wouldn't be a blessing, while others were closer to our previous experience, but we still had no peace about joining. I was beginning to wonder if there was a place for us anywhere. Finally, we visited a church in the town where my parents and sister lived, just up the road, and as soon as we stepped foot inside this place, we all felt at home. We were given a warm and genuine welcome, and instantly felt among friends. We visited for a few weeks and felt we could relate to the pastor and many of the church family. And, most importantly, we felt God was saying he had work for us to do there that would bless the community.

There was no official membership, but we told the pastor and his wife of our commitment to them, and quickly became fully engaged. Initially (after a CRB check) I started helping with children's church as they did not have enough helpers. Then I joined the music team. Mike signed up to help with the PA, and I regularly joined the mid-week prayer meetings too. Our new pastor, Dudley, was unfailingly encouraging, and always spurred us on to use the gifts God had given us.

A while later Dudley approached me and asked me if I would consider becoming an elder. I was shocked. It felt like a real vote of confidence for which I was grateful, but it was also a very real challenge, and it took me a few weeks to pray it through. One of the reasons for my hesitancy was because we had been part of the church for such a relatively short amount of time. But also, until now Mike and I had done pretty much everything ministry-based together. And now I felt somehow disloyal, as if I was somehow betraying him if I accepted a position of leadership without him.

So, I talked to Mike. He wasn't put out at all, though to begin with he was concerned for me about the amount of time it might demand on top of my increasingly busy home education responsibilities. Our eldest was now studying towards GCSE exams, which made home educating a lot more pressured, so he had a point. But I felt that if God was in this, he would help me handle any extra time demands, and as we prayed, it became clear that he really was leading me this way.

From day one I had felt called to support our pastor, and ultimately, I felt God was leading me to this role so I could do just that. Mike agreed and was entirely supportive, having far more confidence in me than I had in myself. I gave Dudley my 'yes' and joined the team.

Of course, despite my fears of being exposed, I wasn't alone. For a start I was joining a team of elders who worked together. They were all older than me, and really encouraging, welcoming me to the team gladly. We were all very different but there was a mutual respect for and appreciation of each other's gifts and personalities. They were wise and experienced, but humble too, and although I felt I hadn't been in the church long enough to understand all the issues, I tended to just ask God about everything, and report back what I felt he was saying, which they seemed to appreciate.

After a while we went on an away day together to pray and plan, and as we sat around the room sharing our thoughts, I suddenly realised: my voice – that I felt had been stolen from me at our previous church – was now being restored.

About two years after joining our new church family, the women of the church were invited to join a ladies' weekend happening nearby. I wasn't usually keen on ladies' meetings – I had always found them a bit twee and patronising – but I wanted to support and encourage those in my church, so I agreed to go. The first meeting was on a Friday evening in October. It was already dark by the time I left home, and the drive was quite stormy. There was a strong wind, whipping up the wet autumn leaves and causing the trees to bend far over. As I drove along the unfamiliar roads, feeling stirred inside by the wild weather outside, I considered how long it had been since I had gone anywhere like this on my own – the voluntary roles I had taken on at church in my spare time were acts of service, but this was somewhere for me to go to receive, with nobody else to be responsible for! Since having children and then embracing their home education, my life had been almost entirely taken over by them. I never resented it for a second – it was the fulfilment of my dreams – but I had to acknowledge that getting quality time to pray or study the Bible had not happened regularly since the birth of my eldest son, now 16 years old. God was still my friend, there was no denying that – I still loved him and sought him when there were important things happening, and I knew he was always with me – but it had been a long time since getting daily, uninterrupted time with him, and I felt a bit dry, spiritually. My children – especially the youngest – were always awake early, and by the time they were all in bed I was usually too exhausted for anything but my own sleep.

So, as I drove through the wind and the rain, not really sure why I was going to the meeting other than wanting to encourage those there, I simply prayed that God would get me there safely and do whatever he wanted that evening. I pulled into the car park, glad to see the warm and welcoming lights shining out of the building.

As I pushed open the door that led to the meeting room, I was instantly overwhelmed. In total contrast to the wild and stormy blackness I had driven through, inside was a haven of beauty and brightness. Joyful music was playing, just loud enough to accompany the happy hum of people chatting and laughing, and the air was filled with the subtle scent of incense and roses. Everywhere I looked were colourful canopies streaming from the rafters, banners of silk declaring God's blessings, and velvet cushions piled in heaps. In each corner of the room there was a richly decorated medieval-style tent containing more silks, piles of cushions, elegant low tables with crystal vases of flowers, and more banners decorated with gold-appliquéd promises of God.

As I caught my breath at the beauty of it all, I noticed some rows of seats, and made my way to sit down. The leader explained that the weekend was about letting the Holy Spirit move wherever he wanted. There would be group worship and prayer, but if at any point we felt we wanted to find a secret, intimate place to go and focus alone on Jesus, we were welcome to use the tents – in fact, to move about however we wanted. There was no sermon that evening, just worship, some prophetic words, and a time of prayer – it was all about simply being with God. I had not been there very long when I began to feel his beautiful presence drawing close. It became so strong, I felt I had been ambushed by his love. At one point I found myself sobbing on the floor – not particularly knowing why, just realising I had been carrying weariness from all the pain and struggles that I had been through for years, doing my best to be faithful to him but without having had much time to spend *with* him. As I cried, I felt the weariness ebb away and the struggles ease, to be replaced by deep peace.

I was being healed of pain that I had not known I was carrying.

On the drive home that night the roads were quiet, the winds and rain having calmed, and I felt cocooned by peace.

The next morning, I drove back to the venue with more anticipation than the night before. Again, we were told not to expect a planned schedule, but just to ask the Holy Spirit how he wanted to lead. We had a beautiful morning of worship, prayer, and encouragement, then after lunch I felt I wanted to get some time on my own with God before everyone gathered in the meeting room again, so I found an empty tent and settled myself on the pile of cushions inside this sanctuary. Surrounded by beauty, with peace flooding my heart, I quickly became aware of God's presence filling the little tent. I looked up, and suddenly noticed the words written on the banner before me: "*As the bridegroom rejoices over the bride, so shall your God rejoice over you.*"[14] I gasped, overcome by the purity and intensity of his love: that he loves us with the same passionate devotion of a bridegroom on his wedding day. I lost track of time as I sat there experiencing wave after wave of his love filling me to overflowing. In my journal I wrote a simple little song that he sang to the deepest parts of my heart.

I am pleased to call you daughter,
I am pleased to call you bride.
I am pleased to have you near me
And to draw you by my side
I delight in your devotion –
the expression of your love.
You're my treasure, now and always,
Come away with me, my love.

The rest of the weekend passed in a beautiful haze of his closeness, and when I got home, I couldn't wait to set an alarm to wake me up before anyone else in the house was up, just to

---

[14] Isaiah 62:5

hang out with God, give him my love and receive his love for me. That pattern continues to this day.

After that weekend I felt renewed, with a fresh ability to focus on my two calls of home educating and leading in the church. However, all was not well in the church. My concern for our pastor had not gone away – if anything, it was intensifying, and I felt God was saying that he needed a sabbatical. There had been some complaining and disagreement in the church, and Dudley had been verbally attacked, putting him under immense strain. As we realised he had not had a break for many years, the other elders all agreed that Dudley needed time off to recover, and we put it to him. He was such a conscientious, diligent man; the responsibility for the church weighed on him heavily, but God was clearly speaking, and he agreed to take three months off. After his return we started some envisioning meetings, hoping for a fresh start. However, despite trying his hardest, it quickly became apparent that the desire and ability to lead were simply no longer in him. And one day, after a team meeting where we tried to work out how to support him, Dudley went home and wrote a resignation letter with immediate effect.

I didn't blame him at all. He shared some time later that God had been speaking to him for a while that his season of pastoring was over, but he was such a diligent man he had found it hard to do something he felt equated to letting people down. Eventually though it just became too much, and he crashed.

This left the elders with a church to lead as a team. A month or two after our pastor resigned, one of the other elders resigned too. Now it was just down to me and one other elder,

Tim, to co-lead. Tim was calm and wise, with experience of leading his own church previously. Neither of us had any ambition to take over; we both shared a desire to follow God's leading, and although we had very different styles, we seemed to complement each other well. I was so grateful for Tim's experience and wisdom during that time. We shared the preaching and booked external preachers whom we trusted. One of these was my old mentor Chris, who became a very strong support for Tim and me, as well as the church.

Although it had only been a year or so since I was asked to be an elder, with all the struggles it had prompted over whether I could do it, here I was now, co-leading a church. Talk about a massive growth journey!

I was lacking in confidence and felt out of my depth…
BUT GOD believed in me and helped me to grow.

CHAPTER 21

A Losing Battle?

One day in Autumn 2019 my sister sent me a text message to say that my dad had gone into hospital because he was having breathing problems. Dad had been dealing with multiple health concerns on and off for many years. Over a decade previously he had undergone brain surgery for the removal of a benign tumour that was messing with his growth hormones. More recently he had been diagnosed with a progressively degenerative disease called PSP (progressive supranuclear palsy), similar to motor neurone disease, and the prognosis was not good. He had also fought with depression for decades, and I was well used to praying for him. Our old issues of my teenage years were well and truly in the past and we had enjoyed a strong, close relationship for decades. He was not a

Christian though, and my main concern was for him to come to know Jesus as his friend – to be spiritually born again, as well as physically healed.

Having received my sister's text, I drove down to the hospital where my dad was waiting for someone to figure out what the problem was so they could treat him. It was apparent quite quickly that his breathing problems were caused by a build-up of fluid in his abdomen that was pressing on his organs. They couldn't initially pin down the reason for the fluid, and frustratingly it took a few days for them to get around to draining it. Eventually they did, and he was sent home, but within 24 hours he had to go back in because the fluid had quickly built up again. This time he was there for weeks.

My sister and I took turns driving my mum to and from the hospital. Dad didn't want any fuss, but Mum wanted to be with him, as did we. She only conceded to one day a week not visiting so that she could rest while one of us three siblings visited. But of course, driving and visiting wasn't all I was doing.

From the first few days when we realised the severity of his condition, I went into battle, praying for a miracle. From the times praying for my babies, I felt I had been trained for spiritual warfare and knew what to do. I prayed, fasted, read God's Bible-promises over my dad, and passionately prayed for him to be saved to eternal life. There were days when I had no words, only tears – and I let them flow as salty liquid-prayers to God. When I asked the Holy Spirit to lead my prayers, I kept sensing I should pray 'light and life' for him. I figured that applied both to his physical healing and his spiritual salvation, so I clung to those words as a promise, and prayed them over and over.

Over the weeks that followed we were dismayed to see our beloved dad, always a towering pillar of strength, deteriorate rapidly. After the second admission to hospital, the medics fitted a permanent drain which helped ease his breathing, but before long he was also struggling to eat. Dad only ever went off his food when he was seriously ill, so it was horrible to watch. Not very long after that he became unsteady on his feet, and after a nasty fall he quickly became too weak to get out of bed. Within another week or two he was very obviously dying. In the first week the oncology team had been brought on board, so we knew we were dealing with cancer, but having had other family members fight cancer over many years, we were not prepared for the aggressiveness of the cancer or the overwhelming rapidity of my dad's decline.

Five weeks after initially going into hospital, and after over a week of having to fight the hospital system to get him released home where he wanted to be, Dad finally came home late one evening at the end of November. Mum asked if I wanted to stay over, but I felt I was needed at home with my boys, and I had peace about that. My sister wanted to be there, and we agreed that she would either call me if the end was near, or we would swap over in the morning. But in the early hours of the next day, I suddenly woke up, and as I listened in the darkness trying to figure out what had woken me, I heard God speak words from the Bible into my heart: "*I am my beloved's and he is mine.*" And I just knew. My dad had been born again right at the end of his earthly life. I don't know how it happened – there's so much we don't know about how God works – but from that point on I knew without a doubt that my much-loved dad now belonged to Jesus.

My sister phoned just minutes later, still in the dark hours before dawn, to urge me to come over. I was already awake so dressed immediately and dashed downstairs, only to discover that my car was frosted over. I scraped it down and set off as quickly as I could but had only been on the road for a minute when my phone rang again. I knew without looking that it could only be my sister, and I knew there could only be one reason for her to call again so quickly, so I just kept driving. I still wanted to be with my mum. Even though I lived only a five-minute drive from my parents, I couldn't get there in time.

My dad had gone to be with his new Saviour.

Of course, I was sad that I had not been there at his moment of passing, but nonetheless I felt a deep peace, because I knew where he was now: striding around Heaven with Jesus; eternally saved, full of joy and peace, and free from all suffering!

Cancer is a hellish, vicious disease that I wouldn't wish on anyone. But even in the aftermath of coming to terms with our loss, those of us whom Dad left behind were deeply grateful that he had been saved from the even more tortuous sentence of PSP that had been hanging over him. It could have taken years of gradually losing the ability to move, then talk, then swallow. Those last five weeks, although brutal, had been long enough to give all of Dad's family the chance to come and say goodbye, but short enough that his suffering had been a very small end to his life. He didn't even need painkillers until the very last night. Those may seem like small mercies, but to those of us who loved him it felt like a real blessing. I still had questions about why he had not been physically healed from *all* his diseases here on earth, as I had prayed – but for now I was comforted by knowing he was free from it all with Jesus.

The weekend after Dad died, I led our church service. Tim was away on a month-long trip that had been planned a long time before anyone resigned, so the church was in my hands. Our church family were fully aware of what I was going through – they had supported my family in prayer and care – and I could feel the strength of their compassionate support on this morning. As I joined in the worship, thanking God in my heart for his presence and peace comforting me, a lady approached whom I had seen there before but who had not been to a meeting for a while. She quietly asked if I would pray for her and explained that she had just been diagnosed with cancer. It was our church custom to pray for people's needs after the service, and, caught off guard, I reassured her that yes, I would either pray at the end or find someone who would, and she went back to her seat. I sat down as the music continued, and was immediately surrounded by self-pitying thoughts: "She obviously doesn't know what you're going through; somebody else should do it," and, "Really you just need to rest and recover before being asked to take on any more warfare," and even, "You just lost a battle against cancer, do you really want to take it on – and lose – again?"

As I heard that final thought flit through my mind, I knew exactly who was speaking, and it wasn't God. It wasn't even me. It was the enemy and he had overplayed his hand.

Immediately the Holy Spirit whispered to my heart, "*Come on, girl, we've got this – you know what to do!*"

I didn't wait a second longer but jumped to my feet and onto the platform. "We're going to pray right now," I announced, "for this dear lady to be healed of cancer." I could see them all looking at me doubtfully, a bit shocked and probably thinking the very same thoughts that had been going through my mind just moments before.

Encouraged by the Holy Spirit, I spoke firmly, saying that I knew they were all aware of what I had just been through, but that we weren't putting our faith in me or my prayers. Our faith was solely in Jesus. They knew I was broken and weak and had absolutely no strength to offer. But in that moment we all remembered that God's strength is best revealed when we are weak. So I laid hands on her[15] and we all prayed in agreement, commanding the cancer to go in Jesus' Name.

There was no way of her knowing if she was instantly healed – she had to go back for scans later to see what was going on. Those scans would show it was shrinking, and a few months later, that it had fully gone! But at the time we just had her faith to go by, and the certainty I felt that Jesus had healed her. I was just so grateful for the opportunity to pray for healing and so glad God encouraged me to keep pursuing victory. I still didn't understand why it seemed to have worked for her and not my dad, but I knew he had it all sorted, even with the questions that remained in me.

In the days running up to my dad's funeral, I woke early one morning before sunrise, feeling an invitation from God to go out for a walk with him. Barney, our dog, was more than happy to accompany me, and we set off to the park. The cold, misty, December air wrapped around us, and we walked in silence through the greyness of early dawn. My heart was raw

[15] *laying on of hands* – The Biblical practice of gently touching someone (usually on their arm or shoulder, or the affected place) while praying for healing

133

and hurting – I was missing my dad terribly, and still unsure why my prayers for physical healing had not been answered as I wanted – and even questioning if I should pray for him to be raised from the dead. I knew he was with Jesus, but I was struggling to find peace.

As I walked, I felt cocooned by the mist, hidden in a secret place with my loving God once more, and I waited for him to speak. As I led Barney up the path to the park entrance, I felt God speak to my heart: "*What do you see, Rachel?*" I admitted that I saw very little – I could only just make out vague shapes of things in the misty half-light. He answered that this is what it is like to live on earth compared to Heaven: as the Bible says, we see 'as through a glass darkly'[16]. We might think we have good natural vision, but even in the full clear light of day, all we see is like vague misty shapes, compared to the stunning vibrant clarity that those in Heaven have. After walking for a while, I eventually came to a bench on a ridge overlooking the park below. I stopped to sit and take in the view: by now the sun had fully risen and burnt off the mist, and there was a glorious light flooding the green field below. Immediately I felt God speak again and say that this was a bit like how it was for my dad now – he was in an infinitely better place, with sharply detailed vision and glorious full revelation. I knew it would be utterly selfish of me to demand that he give it all up just to return to us, and thanked God for showing me that Dad was now truly free, full of life and light as I had been led to pray. And God spoke again and showed me that just as I was overlooking the park from a significant height, so was my dad living in a different, distant realm, watching from above with

---

[16] 1 Corinthians 3:12

the great cloud of witnesses mentioned in the Bible[17], and that one day we would be reunited there in God's presence for all eternity.

My heart was at peace. And what was even more beautiful to me was that when I spoke to my mum about it, God had also been speaking comfort to her through a prayer that somebody had read on TV the same morning, from the festival of *Nine Lessons and Carols*. She had been struck by the portion that read:

> *"Lastly let us remember before God all those who rejoice with us, but* **upon another shore and in a greater light,** *that multitude which no person can number, whose hope was in the Word made flesh, and with whom we for evermore are one..."*[18]

And so God had spoken the same assurance to her grieving heart that he had to mine, and that comfort carried us through the funeral and beyond.

> *I felt utterly defeated and broken...*
> *BUT GOD had the final victory!*

---

[17] Hebrews 12:1
[18] www.sjmp.com/christmas-lessons-and-carols

CHAPTER 22

Full Circle

Shortly after Dad's funeral it was Christmas, but none of the family had the heart to make a huge celebration of it. Instead, we simply gathered quietly, shared happy memories, and took comfort from being together, consoling ourselves that next year would probably be easier. Little did we know that 2020 would bring a whole new realm of challenges!

At the start of the new year Tim mentioned that he felt he should be stepping down in the spring. He had said this before and I wasn't surprised, but I had no idea what would happen – whether I would lead the church on my own, or whether (as I hoped) God would send someone else to lead – but I had to trust that God had a plan. It wasn't just a lack of confidence that left me uncertain. Our congregation were a loving church family who had been kind and supportive of me and mine, especially when my dad died, and we had known many lovely church family times together too. However, there were subtle but obvious disagreements and complaints that had been rumbling for many years, and these seemed to be intensifying.

I worried that my lack of official 'church leader' training was causing me to get things wrong, and I asked God regularly if the complaints (some of which were aimed at me) were valid, but he just kept reminding me he had brought me here for a purpose and to keep following his lead, however it was received. So I did my best to follow him, but just couldn't shake the feeling of being utterly out of my depth, making a mess of things.

There came a Sunday morning when I was leading the congregation in worship. I had been asked to sing more 'good old Pentecostal songs', and asked by others for nothing too loud, nothing too long, nothing too spontaneous... and I felt I had to choose between singing songs that would please God, or pleasing the few who increasingly disagreed over what they all wanted anyway. There was no way of pleasing God *and* everyone there, so I just made it through the songs somehow and then sat down, trying to shake the feeling of impossibility over it all – I just did not know how to meet the demands of the people while obeying God's leading.

I knew I was surrounded by people whom I loved, who had clear gifts and good qualities that I just wanted to encourage, and I tried to focus on the words of our guest speakers that day, but the air felt thick with disapproval and complaints, and however hard I prayed, I felt like I couldn't break through it. Even though I knew most of the people to be lovely and supportive, the few accusations that had been thrown at me over the past year or so seemed to echo all around me: "You must stop prophesying"; "You just want everyone to look at you and make it a Rachel-show"; "I'm leaving if you carry on".

As I tried to battle past the suffocating negativity, I asked God again why he had brought me here. I told him I felt Tim would be a much better person to lead the church, with all his gentle wisdom and experience, but God reminded me he was leading Tim to step down soon. So I asked him again what he was thinking: why had he brought me to this place where I felt I was not achieving anything good... in fact, where I felt I was making things worse?

In response I suddenly saw a vision – a kind of moving mental image, like watching an internal video. In this vision I was standing in open fields that spread far away, and people were milling about across the fields. I was right next to a huge door frame in the middle of these fields, and I was shouting, "Over here!" The people closest to me heard first, and many of them responded and walked through the doorway. There was no door, just the frame, and as they crossed the threshold they disappeared. Somehow I knew they had been transported to a different spiritual dimension – somewhere with more purpose and freedom for them. I shouted louder so those further away could hear. Some responded while others heard and looked my way but chose to continue doing their own thing. I knew in this vision that I was not allowed to leave my place next to the doorway, not to go to others to try to persuade, but just to keep shouting from where I was, to show the way. Eventually, once everyone had heard, I was allowed to go through and follow all those who had heard and responded. And the vision ended.

As I sat and considered the vision, God spoke to my heart clearly to say that this was his plan: *"I brought you here to show people how to find a freer, less religious, and more powerful way of following me. There will be some who will reject it, but I still want to give everyone the opportunity."* So, he had asked me to be someone who would obey him even when others disagreed, who was able to deal with rejection, and who would keep speaking up whether listened to or not.

I was simultaneously comforted (that I was in the right place but not responsible for people's choices as long as I did my part) and challenged (it was nice to know that he believed I was strong enough to handle rejection, but I wasn't so sure myself – it still felt very painful). However, with the reassurance of the vision settled in my heart, I was resolved – I would stay there until he told me everyone had heard and made their choice, and then I would move on too. It no longer mattered so much whether people agreed with me or not (though I still frequently had to check with God if I was messing up his plan). I knew what I was there for and just focused on loving the people and doing my best to show them God's way out of religion.

I was continuing with that goal a short while later in March when the Covid-19 pandemic reached the UK, quickly followed by nationwide lockdown. In terms of not being able to meet with our church family, I was sad to admit that although I dearly loved the people in the congregation and mostly felt loved in return, the element of stress over our Sunday mornings was proving difficult to manage. But now, unable to meet together, we shifted to remote communication, sending encouragements through the post and online instead, as so many church leaders did at the time. Tim stepped back as planned, and I thanked God for a break where I hoped to be able to get a clearer sense of his perspective and vision for when the church could resume meeting.

However, as the weeks and then months passed with no sign of things returning to normal, I realised that I was still experiencing an ongoing sense of relief that was disproportionate to the petty stresses of our mostly lovely congregation. I asked God why I felt such a strong aversion to any idea of going back to meet with our church family. And the more I prayed, the more I came to see that my restlessness was far wider than our little congregation – it was more to do with God's whole church in general. As I chatted with God and wrote down his words, I felt him calling me to something entirely new, that was different to *all* the churches I had ever known and loved.

From the traditional little chapel of my childhood to the close church family of my late teens and early adulthood, then to the faith-filled, dynamic congregations of our ministry years, followed by a brief stop at a sanctuary for healing, and ending up in a church full of lovely people seeking God but stuck in differences of opinion – it had been a rollercoaster ride for sure! I felt we had experienced a broad range of churches, from the ultra-traditional to the wild and free – and as I reviewed them and thanked God for all the many ways he had used churches to bless me and help me to grow in my relationship with him, I had to confess that I had now had enough. Quite simply, I felt stuck in religion – the man-made rules and traditions of church organisations – rather than the simple but powerful relationship with God that Jesus came for. And I was desperate to be set free.

I found myself returning to the question of my childhood: why weren't people getting radically healed and saved like they did when Jesus walked the earth? I also found myself returning to the foundational experiences of my younger days when I simply knew God as my friend. And I just felt sad for how complicated and religious our church meetings had become, compared with that simple but powerful faith.

I longed for the freedom to just be friends with God, and friends with others of his friends, to meet in each other's houses to share meals, to read the Bible and pray together, while seeing people healed and saved daily. No fancy buildings to maintain, no committees or tax-grabbing charity status, no squabbling over styles of worship or length of sermons, no PA desks or segregated children's ministry. Just families and friends eating together, doing life together, and sharing Jesus with their neighbours.

About six months after the initial lockdown, still before the time people were able to properly resume gathering in worship, I realised that God had planted a deep desire in my heart. Church had ceased to be the place of life it used to be for me and had become somewhere stifling. And now, as we moved into the autumn of 2020, I realised God was calling me and my family to choose: were we going to carry on in the old, religious style of churchgoing, or were we going to answer the call to something new – a fresh expression of his original, 2000-year-old plan?

It was only a hard decision to make because I still loved the people in our church and desperately wanted to help them. But God told me that he had a plan for each of them too – that they had heard the message he asked me to bring, and they had made their choices. Now I needed to trust him with them. So, I recorded my last sermon, during which I officially stood down as church leader and member. I was most sad that we couldn't say 'goodbye' in person, but I knew it was time to choose, and God's timing is never wrong, whether we understand it or not. So, we left. I still love the people there – it wasn't about them. It was just about wanting to return, full circle, to the purity of friendship I had as a child when I first encountered God before religion ever had chance to complicate things.

In the couple of years since I stepped down, after spending some time seeking God's plan for us, Mike and I have started a small homegroup where we meet with family (including our own miracle boys) and friends who are also simply friends with God. We share meals, communion; we chat about the Bible and we pray together. We are praying that God will work through us to bring healing and miracles to those around us and are excited about what he has planned for us. It's a small start, but there is life there, and love. And as we continue walking as friends with God, I know he will keep leading us to even better things.

I had come to feel trapped and burdened by religion…
BUT GOD brought me back, full circle, to the simple
friendship of my childhood.

CHAPTER 23

He Wants to be Known (Writing the Book)

So here we are – at the end of the book, having visited many of the points of my life where God showed his faithful friendship, in many ways.

I hope that you can see that although the book has been written about my life, because that's what I know, when God chose to be friends with me it wasn't because I am someone 'special'. I am no more or less special than any other individual on the face of the earth. We are all unique, all special in God's eyes, and he wants to be friends with us all. Your friendship with him will probably look different to mine because you are different, exactly as he wants – he loves difference and variety! I have received some miracles that others have not – but then some have received miracles that I have not.

It's not about comparison, just each person learning to grow
in their own friendship with him. I have been blessed with
several encounters of tangibly feeling God's presence with me,
and I'm grateful for those. They make good stories too, but as
you can hopefully see, they are few and far between. Most of
my life has been about simply walking with God in the prosaic,
everyday-ness of life, and that's good and as it should be. It's
not about comparing your everyday to my highlights – it's just
about showing what a good and faithful friend God is to
anyone who would like his friendship.

Many times while writing this book I found myself doubting
its purpose. There are so many good books out there – so many
truly inspiring accounts of radical conversions and outstanding
miracles – and my life seemed small and foolish in comparison.
I also wondered what the point was of exposing my private life,
either risking ridicule and rejection, or making myself look
better than I am, causing people to compare themselves
unfavourably.

And the longer I worked on the book, re-writing and re-
writing to improve the clunky or waffly parts, the more I
doubted my own ability to write well. At times I was convinced
that I didn't have it in me to write the kind of book that would
do God justice. The pitfalls seemed endless. But the thing that
kept me writing through it all was a single, short conversation
that I had with God a few years ago…

As usual I had got up early in the morning to pray, to hang
out with God in the peace and quiet before the rest of the family
got up. I was in the habit of chatting with God about all sorts
of things – sometimes I would sit in silence and enjoy his
company, sometimes I would ask for help, pour out my

struggles, or ask questions, and sometimes he would share his thoughts with me.

That morning as I prayed, I started to feel God pouring waves of love into me. It wasn't something I felt with my physical senses, but was like an internal, spiritual awareness of his light and powerful love that overwhelmed everything else. It became so intense I could hardly bear it. My surroundings – the comfy sofa, the dog dozing at my feet, the low light of dawn, the worship music playing softly on my laptop – all faded into irrelevance as I slipped to my knees, choked and brought to tears by God's immense and undeserved kindness. And there I blurted out something that I immediately wanted to take back, feeling it was the stupidest thing I had ever said. I asked, "God, what can I do for you?"

Yep – stupid. As if a flawed little created being like me could ever do anything for the one who made me: all-mighty, all-powerful, all-present God! But in that split second of feeling utterly foolish and embarrassed, I heard God answer immediately – not in ridicule but with the most intense longing in his voice. It sounded – could it be true? – like he was grateful to me for asking!

And he answered, "*I want to be known.*"

People seem to think God cares most about whether we keep his rules, attend church and do our best to be good people. And yes, he sees it all and does care about it all, because he cares about us. But that day I realised with crystal clarity that there is one thing he cares about more than any of that: he simply wants us to KNOW him. Not know *about* him, like learning theory about some historical or famous person you've never met – but to truly know him as a close friend. He's not after religion, but relationship with us. It's what we were created for. He wants to be known – not just by me, but by you too. He's not waiting for you to make yourself holy, perfect, committed, or good enough. The truth is that on our own this is impossible: we are all flawed, and we can never make ourselves good enough. That's why God sent his perfect Son to make the way for us to be restored to friendship with him. Through Jesus we can all be friends with God. That's the Gospel – the good news that he came to share.

And so here I am, writing this book in the hope that as you have read some of the stories from my life so far, you have come to know a bit of the incredible love, goodness, kindness, and amazing friendship of God. On my own I'm no more or less special than you. But some of my life truly has been amazing, simply because I am friends with an amazing God. And you can be too – he's just waiting for you to ask.

If you'd like to get to know God as your friend, just ask him. It's what he's waiting for. Don't worry about understanding everything – I didn't at first. Just remember God loves you and wants you to get to know him in mutual friendship. Please don't struggle alone like I did for so long, though – we all need friends to help us on the journey. Make sure you connect with other Christians for help in getting to know God better. If you have any Christian friends, chat to them, and let them know what you're thinking, and maybe ask them to share *their* story of friendship with God. Alternatively, you could find an Alpha[19] course, either local or online: they can be a great place to start connecting.

---

[19] https://alpha.org.uk/try

Or you can reach me at:
www.rachelyarworthwriter.wordpress.com
I'd love to hear from you!

*On our own, we are all flawed and broken, lost in
sin...*
*BUT GOD through Jesus has made a way for us to be
friends with Him, for all eternity.*

Printed in Great Britain
by Amazon

34759744R00091